Virgin VEGAN EVERYDAY RECIPES ❤ for Satisfying your Appetite

DONNA KELLY and ANNE TEGTMEIER

GIBBS SMITH
TO ENRICH AND INSPIRE HUMANKIND

For Kate Kelly and Neil Ransom, Donna's daughter and son-in-law
and Anne's sister and brother-in-law, in honor of their creative culinary
adventurousness. Long live their Passionate International Gastronomer
(P.I.G.) Project!

First Edition
17 16 15 14 13   5 4 3 2 1

Text © 2013 Donna Kelly and Anne Tegtmeier
Photographs © 2013 Susan Barnson Hayward

Published by
Gibbs Smith
P.O. Box 667
Layton, Utah 84041

1.800.835.4993 orders
www.gibbs-smith.com

Designed by AJB Design
Printed and bound in China

Gibbs Smith books are printed on either recycled, 100% post-consumer
waste, FSC-certified papers or on paper produced from sustainable PEFC-
certified forest/controlled wood source. Learn more at www.pefc.org.

Library of Congress Cataloging-in-Publication Data

Kelly, Donna, 1955-
  Virgin vegan everyday recipes : for satisfying your appetite /
Donna Kelly and Anne Tegtmeier. — First Edition.
      pages cm
  Includes index.
  ISBN 978-1-4236-2522-3
1. Vegan cooking. I. Tegtmeier, Anne. II. Title.
TX837.K375 2013
641.5'636—dc23
                          2012033145

Contents

ACKNOWLEDGMENTS

Donna and Anne would like to thank Jim Kelly for his natural gift for food photography; much appreciation to Michelle Branson and the editorial staff of Gibbs Smith; much obliged to Kimberly James for her vegetarian Southern cuisine expertise; many thanks to Peter and Chrizelle Ransom for their recipe tasting and testing; and gratitude to all the Kellys for their tireless taste testing. Special thanks to Sandra Hoopes, Donna's sister and Anne's aunt, for her "cheffy" culinary mentoring.

We also want to thank all the regular readers at our blog, www.apron stringsblog.com. You inspire us anew every day.

TIPS, TRICKS, AND TECHNIQUES

INTRODUCTION TO VEGAN COOKING

We decided to write a vegan cookbook for everyone: something vegans would love, of course, but full of delicious and accessible recipes that would appeal to nonvegans, too, no matter what their personal health needs might be. These are nutrient-rich dishes that can serve as the foundation of a strictly vegan diet, and will also benefit anyone looking to increase the amount of plant-based food sources in their dietary repertoire.

We also wanted to avoid overusing prepackaged, processed-food substitutes as much as possible, such as soy cheeses and faux meat products. You'll find a few exceptions for certain fun and indulgent recipes, but we primarily based our recipes on whole foods. (We all need some conveniences and short-cuts from time to time, of course!)

We are not strictly vegans ourselves, but over the years we have each spent a lot of time exploring vegetarian and vegan cooking, both for ourselves and for our loved ones. Along the way, we found that we really enjoyed the results of our experiments—both in our palates and in our healthy choices. We're happy to share these with you and yours.

Before we get started, here's a brief guide to some ingredients you'll find useful in the upcoming recipes. Some may be familiar already, some perhaps not yet, but we've taken care to make sure these are ones you'll find available in most grocery stores. In today's ever-more-sophisticated food world, this is becoming easier and easier as stores which used to be considered specialty niche markets are now in practically every neighborhood, and almost all mainstream stores have risen to the challenge by developing impressive natural sections.

Bulk foods: Natural/health food stores have long made extensive bulk foods sections a cornerstone of their market, and now many conventional stores have adopted the practice as well. Many common staples are available in bulk form, which is usually far more economical as well as being environmentally friendly. We encourage you to explore the bulk food departments available to you. Quite a few of the ingredients we use in our recipes come from the bulk section.

A word on nuts in particular: if you've never tried getting your nuts from here, rather than the tiny and expensive packages in the baking department or in the canisters in the snack food aisle, we definitely suggest you try it! This is also the best place to find raw nuts. You can then roast them yourself to your own preference, or soak them if the recipe calls for it or if you prefer to do so for nutritional reasons.

Coconut milk: This has become more and more widely available in recent years, and can be found in a number of forms. It is available in cans, often in the Asian section of your grocery store, and comes in both regular and light varieties. It is also frequently available in shelf-stable quart boxes, just like many brands of soy, almond, and other nondairy milk (see below) are. In some stores, it is also available in the refrigerated dairy section in half-gallon containers. Coconut milk yogurt and ice cream are now also popular; So Delicious is one dependable brand which certainly lives up to its name.

In our cookbook, you may use either the regular or the light variety unless we specifically state the recommended type.

Other alternative milks: In addition to soy and rice milk, almond, hemp, oat, and even hazelnut milk have become very widely available, and most come in a few flavors in addition to unsweetened plain. All are versatile and suitable for a variety of uses; hemp milk is particularly nutritious. Experiment according to your own needs and preferences. When our recipes call for a certain kind of milk, we do recommend trying it with that type of milk the first time you make it, but if you have food sensitivities or allergies, or simply have another kind more readily available, feel free to substitute another kind.

Coconut oil: This is a staple to add to your pantry ASAP! It is available in both regular and virgin varieties. Coconut oil is one of the healthiest sources of saturated fat as it contains MCFAs (Medium Chain Fatty Acids) which have no negative effect on cholesterol and helps protect against heart disease. A growing number of other health benefits are attributed to coconut oil, including topical use on your skin. The virgin form even possesses antibacterial properties.

It is very heat stable with a long shelf life. It is especially good for cooking at high temperatures unlike some other oils that break down at far lower points. You'll see that we use it often in our baked goods, too. For those who like the flavor of coconut, the virgin form has more coconut flavor, but for those who want the health benefit with a much milder taste, the regular variety will be preferable.

Butter substitutes: There are two primary kinds of substitutes we use for butter in recipes where oil (olive or coconut) will not work. We also recommend using nonhydrogenated products whenever possible. Organic palm shortening (Spectrum Organics has a great one) is a nonhydrogenated shortening that's particularly good for baking needs. Earth Balance Spread is another brand that can be counted on to be both vegan (not all margarines are—check the label for whey and lactose) and is also free of trans fats.

Nutritional yeast: This is available in natural food stores as well as most natural food sections in conventional grocery stores. It may be sold in bulk or in a package (Bragg's is one popular brand). This deactivated yeast is light yellow in color and can have either a flaky or powdery appearance; either one is fine. Nutritional yeast is popular among vegans as it not only adds a cheesy flavor to many recipes (it's a key ingredient in the classic dairy-free "cheese" sauce), it also adds essential B vitamins in addition to contributing other minerals, protein, and fiber.

Chocolate: Is chocolate vegan? It most definitely can be, as long as you're careful about checking the source. You're looking for dairy-free, whey-free, and casein-free. Milk chocolate, of course, is not, but many semisweet, bittersweet, and especially dark chocolates are. Checking your labels is always important, but some trusted dairy-free brands include Enjoy Life, Dagoba, Green and Black, Newman's Own, and Sunspire, as well as Trader Joe's chocolate chips.

Sweeteners: Sugar isn't an animal product—therefore it must be vegan, right? Well, yes and no. Sugar itself is not derived from animals, but the methods used to process many mainstream brands of sugar may not be vegan friendly (some varieties are made using "bone char"). Your best bet is to go for labels that use the following terminology: evaporated cane juice, unrefined cane sugar, beet sugar, raw sugar, and, of course, vegan sugar.

Other sugar substitutes with possible health benefits that you may want to experiment with include maple syrup, raw agave nectar, coconut sugar, date sugar, and brown rice syrup. (Note that honey is not vegan, as it is most definitely derived from animals.)

Agar agar: Jell-O may not be vegan, but that doesn't mean you can't enjoy recipes that normally include gelatin. Agar agar is actually a seaweed product that packs a powerful gelling punch (trust us, a little goes a long way). These white flakes are carried in both natural and Asian grocery stores. It is sometimes found with baking needs, but may be found alongside other seaweed products (like the kelp, kombu, and the nori sheets that are used to make sushi) in the Asian section of the international foods aisle.

Tofu: We literally wrote the book on tofu! (Our first collaboration was *101 Things To Do With Tofu,* Gibbs Smith, 2007). This high-protein bean curd originated in Asia and comes in four basic varieties: firm, extra-firm, soft, and silken (not to be confused with soft). Firm is the most commonly available and the most widely used. The most popular brands, and the ones that are used in these recipes, come packaged in water. Most general supermarkets now carry tofu in their produce sections, while natural and specialty grocery stores may carry it in or near the dairy cases.

Some recipes call for tofu that has been frozen and then thawed. This process triggers a change in the texture of the tofu, making it more chewy and easy to crumble. When frozen, the moisture within the tofu separates from the bean curd, making it easier to squeeze all excess water out. The tofu is now spongy and porous, ideal for absorbing flavors. Tofu can be frozen in its own water or drained and wrapped in plastic until ready to use. Depending on how you plan to use it, tofu can be cut into slabs or cubes before freezing, or it can be frozen whole.

Recipes commonly call for tofu to be drained and/or pressed. All that draining tofu requires is simply pouring off the excess water from the container. To press excess moisture out from within the tofu, a number of easy techniques can be used. One method calls for wrapping the brick of tofu in dish towels then setting something heavy on top of it (like a large glass jar). A faster method is to sandwich it between two plates and gently press, pouring off the water that emerges. If a recipe calls for the tofu to be crumbled, you can wrap it in dish towels and wring the towels out over the sink, both squeezing the moisture out and crumbling the block of tofu. This works for both regular, refrigerated tofu, and for tofu that has been frozen and then thawed.

Soy cheese/cream cheese: We don't use many substitutes in our recipes as we wanted to focus on whole and unprocessed foods for the most part, but there are times when a little bit of substitute can be both delicious and helpful. You can find these in both natural foods stores and in conventional supermarkets; in the former, as with tofu, they tend to be kept in the dairy case, while in the latter they might also be found in or adjacent to the produce department. Please read your labels carefully; some brands that don't specifically label themselves as "vegan" may say "soy cheese" but will also contain casein, a no-no for vegans or anyone avoiding dairy.

Tempeh and seitan: Tempeh and seitan are two other foods frequently used as meat substitutes. We don't use them here in our cookbook, but they are items that you may encounter as you explore the world of vegan cooking. Tempeh is made from fermented soybeans. While it is a relative of tofu, the texture and taste are completely different. It's especially good in stir-fries or stews. Seitan, not a soy product, is instead made from wheat gluten and has a chewy, meaty texture. It is available commercially, but can also be made at home with vital wheat gluten.

See **www.virginvegan.com** for more information about veganism, resources, videos, and more recipes.

VEGAN STAPLES

We wanted to include a few simple recipes for homemade vegan condiments, sauces, and staples. They're easy to make and good to have on hand, whether for use in the dishes in our cookbook or in any other recipe you like. We think you'll find that they're much less expensive and much tastier than their store-bought counterparts—not to mention far less processed.

Vegetable Broth

Makes 8 cups

This homemade version is simple to make and more fresh and flavorful than many store-bought broths. Make up a batch and keep some handy in your fridge!

2 large carrots, peeled and sliced into ¼-inch pieces
1 large onion, peeled and cut into 8 chunks
2 celery stalks, cut into ½-inch slices, leaves included
2 tablespoons olive oil
3 cloves garlic, peeled and smashed
10 white button mushrooms, quartered
1 small bunch parsley (about 20 sprigs), roughly chopped
2 teaspoons salt *
1 teaspoon cayenne pepper sauce
2 teaspoons pepper
3 bay leaves
8 cups water

Brown the carrots, onion, and celery in oil in a large stockpot over medium-high heat, about 3 minutes. Add remaining ingredients and reduce heat to a simmer. Cook for 20 minutes. Turn off heat and let cool to warm then strain. Keep refrigerated in an airtight container up to 1 week.

* For a darker and more robust stock, delete the salt and add 2 tablespoons soy sauce.

Vegan Whipped Cream

Makes 2 cups

This has the taste and texture of real whipped cream with a slight hint of coconut flavor.

> 1 can (13 ounces) regular coconut milk (not light)
> 3 tablespoons powdered sugar
> 1 teaspoon vanilla
> Pinch of salt

Chill the can of coconut milk for several hours, or overnight. Open can and, with a spoon, carefully remove the top layer of solidified coconut cream (it will be about half of the can). Reserve remaining liquid for another use.

Whip the solidified cream at high speed with all remaining ingredients until the consistency of whipped cream, about 3 minutes. Can be stored in refrigerator for about 8 hours.

Vegannaise

Makes 1½ cups

The comfort feel and taste of mayo—and dairy free!

> 1 cup silken tofu
> 2 tablespoons lemon juice
> 1 teaspoon dry mustard
> ¼ teaspoon salt
> 2 tablespoons extra virgin olive oil
> Dash of cayenne pepper sauce

Blend all ingredients in a blender until very smooth. Store in refrigerator in airtight container for up to 2 weeks.

Vegan Pesto

Makes 1½ cups

This enlightened version of the Italian classic sauce is so packed with flavor; you'll forget it's good for you too!

> 3 cups fresh basil leaves
> ½ cup chopped walnuts
> 2 tablespoons nutritional yeast
> ½ cup extra virgin olive oil
> Salt and pepper, to taste

Whirl the basil, nuts, and yeast in food processor until leaves are in small bits. Slowly stream in oil while processing until mixture becomes a smooth purée. Add salt and pepper.

Sweet and Spicy Asian Dipping Sauce

Makes 1 cup

Perfect tang and sweetness for dipping spring rolls or tempura veggies.

> 1 Serrano pepper, thinly sliced
> 1 clove garlic, pressed
> 1 tablespoon grated fresh ginger
> ⅔ cup hot water
> 3 tablespoons sugar
> Juice and zest from 1 lime
> 1 tablespoon soy sauce
> 1 teaspoon sesame oil

Stir all ingredients together and let stand about 20 minutes. Strain and serve.

Tangy Spiced Ketchup

Makes 1 cup

> 1 clove garlic, minced
> ½ tablespoon coconut or olive oil
> 1 cup ketchup
> ½ teaspoon red pepper flakes
> ½ teaspoon chili powder
> Dash of cayenne pepper sauce

Sauté garlic in oil over medium heat for about 2–3 minutes. Stir in ketchup and spices; adjust seasoning to taste. Serve warm or refrigerated.

Almond Ricotta and Almond Sour Cream

Makes about 2 cups Ricotta and about 3 cups Sour Cream

You won't believe how close these vegan versions are to the originals—until you taste them!

ALMOND RICOTTA

> 1 cup (5 ounces) blanched slivered almonds
> 1½ cups water
> ¼ teaspoon salt
> 1 tablespoon lemon juice
> 1 tablespoon extra virgin olive oil

Blend all ingredients in food processor or blender, just until small bits, about 20 seconds. Do not purée until smooth.

Simmer in a saucepan until thickened, about 3–5 minutes, stirring frequently. Let cool. Use chilled or at room temperature.

ALMOND SOUR CREAM

Increase water to 2 cups and lemon juice to 3 tablespoons. When blending mixture, blend until a very smooth purée, about 2 minutes, in a blender.

Eggplant Bacon

Makes about 12 strips

Smokey, salty, browned strips of deliciousness—that won't clog your arteries!

1 baby eggplant or Japanese eggplant
4 tablespoons low-sodium tamari or soy sauce
1 tablespoon maple syrup
1 teaspoon liquid smoke
Canola oil spray

Cut eggplant into ¼-inch thick strips lengthwise and then into 1-inch wide strips, without skin. Toss strips with tamari, syrup, and liquid smoke. Refrigerate for about 2 hours.

Place strips on a baking sheet lined with a silicone baking mat or parchment paper that has been lightly sprayed with oil. Brush with a little of liquid marinade. Spray tops of strips lightly with oil.

Bake for 10 minutes. Turn strips over and brush with marinade. Bake another 10 minutes. Continue baking in 5 minute increments, turning every 5 minutes, watching very closely as you go so as not to burn.

Strips are done when they are lightly browned all over with very dark brown spots. Remove from oven and let cool. Strips will harden as they cool.

Perfect Pie Crust

Makes 1 (8-inch) double crust or 2 (8-inch) single crusts

This easy, tasty all-purpose crust recipe makes enough for a double crust, good for sweet and savory fillings alike!

3 cups flour
1 teaspoon sugar
1 teaspoon salt
⅔ cup palm shortening
¾ cup ice water

Whisk the flour, sugar, and salt together and transfer to food processor. Scatter spoonfuls of the shortening over the top and pulse just until mixture resembles coarse sand. Add in half the ice water and pulse again, adding a little more just until a dough ball begins to form.

Place dough on a floured surface and shape it into a ball. Divide ball in half and roll each half out into a disc that's about 1 inch thick. Wrap each half in plastic wrap and refrigerate for 1 hour.

When ready to bake, roll out between two sheets of wax paper and bake as directed. If you're not planning on a top crust, you can still roll the second half out, press it into a pie pan, then rewrap it and pop it in the freezer for easy future use.

BOUNTIFUL BREAKFASTS

Pineapple Upside-Down Pancakes
Makes 8 pancakes

The classic American dessert made vegan—and in pancake form.

3 ripe bananas
2 ¼ cups vanilla almond milk or soy milk, divided
1½ cups whole-grain flour (such as wheat or oat)
2 teaspoons baking powder
½ teaspoon salt
1 small pineapple
Canola oil spray

Mash bananas with a fork—you should have 1½ cups. Blend the bananas with about ½ cup of milk until smooth. Blend in remaining milk.

Whisk together flour, baking powder, and salt. Stir into banana mixture until blended. Set aside while cooking pineapple slices.

Cut outer skin off pineapple. Cut pineapple into 8 (½-inch thick) slices. Using a small cookie cutter, remove center core of each slice. Warm a skillet to medium-low heat and then spray skillet with a little oil. Cook 3 or 4 pineapple slices for about 2 minutes.

Turn pineapple slices over. Immediately pour ¼ cup batter into center of each pineapple slice, allowing batter to spill over and form a circle around outside of pineapple slice. Add a little more batter if necessary to form a pancake. Cook for 2–3 minutes, until lightly browned.

Carefully flip over and cook other side for about 2 minutes, until pancake is cooked through and is lightly browned. Repeat the process with remaining pineapple and batter.

Multi-Grain Muesli Pancakes

Makes 12 medium-size pancakes

The flavor and texture of these multi-grain pancakes is so incredible that you will want to keep the dry ingredients mixed up and ready to go for breakfast, lunch, or dinner

> 3 cups muesli cereal (makes 1½ cups ground)
> 1⅓ cups whole-grain flour (such as wheat or oat)
> 1 tablespoon baking powder
> 1 teaspoon salt
> 1 teaspoon baking soda
> 1 tablespoon flax seed meal, softened in 3 tablespoons
>   boiling water
> 4 tablespoons vegan margarine, melted
> 3 cups vanilla soy milk or almond milk
> 1 tablespoon lemon juice
> Water, as needed

Pulse the muesli in food processor until cereal is very small crumbs. Stir together the dry ingredients. (At this point, you may keep mix in an airtight container for up to 3 weeks in the pantry or 2 months in the refrigerator. It will last a year or more in the freezer.)

Mix together the flax seed, margarine, milk, and lemon juice. Mix the dry ingredients with the wet ingredients. Let stand 10 minutes. Add water as necessary to thin to a pancake batter consistency.

Heat a skillet or griddle to medium heat. Add a little oil to skillet and then pour batter into pan, forming circles about ¼ inch thick. Cook for 1–2 minutes, until lightly browned. Turn pancakes over and cook another minute or so, until lightly browned and cooked through. Repeat until batter is gone.

Rise and Shine · Citrus Smoothie

Makes 2 servings

Wake up your taste buds drinking this smoothie with a zing!

½ mango, peeled and diced
¼ cup frozen orange juice concentrate
1 tablespoon grated fresh ginger
Juice and zest of 1 lime
Pinch of salt
16 ounces silken tofu
¼ cup agave nectar or maple syrup, or
    more to taste
Ice cubes, as desired

Place all ingredients except ice cubes in a blender in the listed order. Blend until very smooth. While blender is on, add ice cubes, a few at a time, until you reach the consistency you like.

Dairy-Free French Toast

Makes 4 servings

You won't believe this classic French breakfast dish is just as delicious without dairy—until you try it.

½ cup silken tofu
1 cup vanilla almond milk
½ teaspoon cinnamon
¼ teaspoon turmeric
Pinch of salt
8 slices stale dairy-free bread
Vegetable oil

Blend all ingredients together except bread and oil in a blender and then pour into a pie pan. Warm a skillet to medium heat and then add a little oil to pan.

Soak bread slices in milk mixture, one at a time. Place in pan and cover and cook about 2 minutes on each side, until lightly browned. Serve warm with syrup or desired toppings.

Sunrise Sweet Potato Hash Browns

Makes 4–6 servings

These have a touch of Caribbean flair to them—spice them up to your heart's content!

1 tablespoon coconut or olive oil
2 large sweet potatoes (garnet variety), peeled and shredded
1 medium onion, thinly sliced
1 teaspoon salt
1 red bell pepper, diced
3 cloves garlic, minced
½ cup packed cilantro, finely chopped
⅓ cup unsweetened shredded coconut
Juice and finely grated zest of 1 lime
Tangy Spiced Ketchup (page 13)

Heat oil in a large skillet over medium-high heat. Add sweet potatoes, onion, and salt; cook, stirring frequently, until sweet potatoes start to soften, about 3–5 minutes. Add bell pepper and garlic, incorporate thoroughly, and cook for another 4–5 minutes, stirring, until the sweet potatoes are just starting to brown a bit.

Stir in cilantro, coconut, lime juice, and zest and cook for another 2–3 minutes. Serve with Tangy Spiced Ketchup.

Very Veggie Breakfast Burritos

Makes 8 servings

These will transport you to a sunny morning on a California beach—and give you energy to hit the waves!

> 4 tablespoons olive oil, divided
> 1 yellow onion, diced
> 1 carrot, diced
> 1 stalk celery, diced
> 14 ounces firm or extra-firm tofu, pressed and crumbled
> 1 teaspoon turmeric
> 2 teaspoons cumin
> 1 tablespoon balsamic vinegar
> 1 tablespoon tamari or soy sauce
> 1 red bell pepper, chopped
> ¼ cup chopped green onion
> 1 can (20 ounces) black beans, drained and rinsed
> 1 teaspoon chili powder
> 8 medium flour tortillas
> 1 large avocado, cubed
> Salsa, optional

In a large skillet, sauté onion in 2 tablespoons oil until softened, about 2 minutes. Add carrot and celery and sauté 3 more minutes. Mix in tofu, spices, vinegar, and tamari; continue stirring for 3–4 more minutes. Set aside.

In another large skillet, sauté bell pepper and green onion in remaining oil over medium heat until softened, 2–3 minutes. Add black beans and chili powder and cook another 2–3 minutes. Stir in the scrambled tofu mixture and remove from heat.

Spoon a heaping ½ cup of the tofu and veggie mixture down the center of each tortilla then top with a few cubes of the avocado. Roll up, folding ends in. Serve with salsa, if desired.

Lilybars

Makes about 8 bars

Named after Anne's daughter and Donna's granddaughter in homage to the popular Larabar, these easy, delicious, nutrition-packed raw energy bars will be a hit with adults and kids alike! They're fun to make and so much more budget friendly than the store-bought brands.

CHOCOLATE CHIP COOKIE DOUGH LILYBARS

1 cup pitted and roughly chopped Medjool dates
¾ cup raw cashews
2 tablespoons dairy-free chocolate chips or cacao nibs
Dash of cinnamon, optional

Place the dates in a food processor. Pulse until processed to a paste; the dates will start to form a ball. Transfer paste to a medium bowl (no need to clean the processor).

Add the cashews to the processor and pulse until finely chopped. You definitely want this fine, but you don't want to go too far and make cashew butter. Add the nuts to the bowl with the date paste and add chocolate chips. Use your fingers to knead the nuts into the paste. Once well combined, roll into a log.

Place a sheet of plastic wrap in an 8-inch loaf pan with enough to hang over each end. Transfer the log to the loaf pan and press mixture evenly into the bottom of the pan. Then lift it out, using the extra plastic wrap to help. Divide into 8 bars. Wrap tightly and refrigerate any leftover bars.

Try experimenting with different varieties, maybe adding some flax and oats, maybe some spices. The ratio is approximately 1 cup dates (or a combination of dates and other moist dried fruits) to ¾ cup nuts to make the foundation and then take it from there.

Here are some variations to get you started.

1 cup pitted and roughly chopped whole Medjool dates
¼ cup dried apricots
1 cup raw almonds
¼ cup dried blueberries

CRANBERRY OR GOJI BERRY PECAN LILYBARS

1 cup pitted and roughly chopped Medjool dates
⅓ cup raw cashews
⅓ cup raw pecans
¼ cup dried cranberries or goji berries
1 to 2 teaspoons orange zest

All flavor combinations use the same basic steps as in the first version: Process dates and other moist fruits first, then nuts, then transfer to a bowl, add additional mix-ins, combine together, and press into bars using a loaf pan and plastic wrap.

Country-Style Grits

Makes 4–6 servings

This is real Southern comfort—no cheese or cream required!

2 cups Vegetable Broth (page 10)
1 cup unsweetened almond milk
1 cup grits or coarsely ground cornmeal
2 teaspoons salt
½ teaspoon freshly ground pepper
2 tablespoons nutritional yeast
Cayenne pepper sauce, to taste

Bring broth and almond milk to a boil then whisk in grits. Add salt and pepper, reduce heat to low, cover, and let simmer for 30 minutes, stirring occasionally. Stir in nutritional yeast and cayenne pepper sauce and serve.

Smothered Biscuits with Country Gravy

Makes 6–8 biscuits

A hearty bit of down-home heaven is in this savory Southern breakfast.

1½ cups flour
2 tablespoons baking powder
½ teaspoon salt
½ cup chilled coconut oil
2 tablespoons maple syrup
½ cup almond milk

Preheat oven to 375 degrees. Stir together flour, baking powder, and salt in a large bowl. Scatter the coconut oil over the flour mixture in about 8 small spoonfuls. With a pastry cutter, incorporate the coconut oil. Add maple syrup and almond milk and stir until a ball is formed. Lightly flour a work area and rolling pin. Knead the dough for about 2 minutes and then roll out until about ½ inch thick.

Using a 3-inch biscuit cutter (or rim of a glass), cut out as many circles as you can, placing biscuits on a baking sheet lined with parchment paper or a silicone mat. Repeat rolling and cutting until dough is used up. Bake for 10–12 minutes, until lightly golden on the top.

COUNTRY GRAVY

3 tablespoons toasted sesame oil
3 tablespoons flour
2 cups unsweetened almond milk
1 tablespoon tamari or soy sauce
1½ teaspoons smoked paprika
¼ cup nutritional yeast
½ teaspoon each salt and freshly ground pepper
2 to 3 dashes hot pepper sauce

In a saucepan, warm the sesame oil over medium heat. Add flour and cook for 4–5 minutes, whisking frequently. Stir in almond milk and tamari, continuing to whisk until mixture starts to thicken. Add remaining seasonings. Pour over fresh biscuits and serve hot.

Joyful Almond Oatmeal

Makes 4–6 servings

This is a heavenly combination of flavors—like a popular coconut almond candy bar in a breakfast bowl.

> 1½ cups steel-cut oats
> 4 cups vanilla almond milk
> 1 cup water
> ½ teaspoon salt
> 1 cup sweetened shredded coconut
> ½ cup sliced almonds
> 3 tablespoons coconut oil
> ½ cup currants or diced raisins, optional

Toast the oats in a dry skillet over medium-high heat until browned and fragrant; about 2–3 minutes. Place the oats, almond milk, water, and salt in a slow cooker. Cook covered on low heat for 7–8 hours; or high heat for 3–4 hours.

Spread coconut and almonds in a single layer on a baking sheet covered with parchment paper or a silicone mat. Broil for 5 minutes about 6 inches from the heat, stirring once halfway through. Then check every minute and bake until coconut and almonds turn a light brown, about 8 minutes total cooking time. Stir coconut, almonds, coconut oil, and currants into oatmeal. Serve warm.

SOUPS AND STEWS

Veggie Gumbo
Makes 10–12 servings

The bold flavors of the bayou come through loud and clear in this vegan version of the classic gumbo. *Les bon temps roulez!*

⅓ cup peanut oil
⅓ cup flour
2 green bell peppers, finely chopped
2 large onions, finely chopped
3 stalks celery, finely chopped
4 cloves garlic, minced
14 ounces firm tofu, pressed and cut into ½-inch cubes
8 cups Vegetable Broth (page 10)
1 pound frozen sliced okra
1 can (15 ounces) diced tomatoes
2 bay leaves
½ teaspoon thyme
½ teaspoon each cayenne pepper and hot pepper sauce
2 teaspoons Liquid Smoke
1 teaspoon salt
Freshly ground pepper, to taste
1 teaspoon gumbo filé, optional
Hot cooked rice

Combine oil and flour over medium heat in large cast iron pot or Dutch oven. Cook, stirring continuously, until it turns a rich golden blonde color, about 15–20 minutes. Add the bell peppers, onions, celery, and garlic, and keep stirring until vegetables are coated with flour mixture and begin to soften. Add tofu and stir into mixture.

Add broth and raise heat to high. Add the okra, tomatoes, bay leaves, and all seasonings. Lower heat and allow to simmer for 45 minutes. Remove bay leaves and serve with rice and additional hot pepper sauce, to taste.

Ultimate Veggie Chili

Makes 8–10 servings

This recipe was featured on the first season of Food Network's Ultimate Recipe Showdown. We bet you'll think it's the best veggie chili you've ever had, too!

1 yellow onion, chopped
1 red bell pepper, chopped
3 cloves garlic, minced
2 tablespoons olive oil
1 tablespoon ground cumin
1 teaspoon chipotle chili powder
1 teaspoon crushed red pepper flakes
14 ounces extra-firm tofu, frozen and thawed
2 cans (14 ounces each) diced tomatoes, with liquid
1 can (28 ounces) crushed tomatoes
1 can (4 ounces) diced jalapeños, drained
1 can (4 ounces) green chiles, drained
2 cans (14 ounces each) black beans, drained and rinsed
1 can (14 ounces) dark kidney beans, drained and rinsed
1 cup fresh or frozen corn
1 cup whole roasted cashews, diced
Salt and freshly ground pepper, to taste

In a large stockpot, sauté onion, bell pepper, and garlic in oil over medium-high heat until onion starts to soften. Stir in cumin, chipotle powder, and red pepper flakes. Crumble tofu into the mixture and sauté 5 minutes more.

Reduce heat to medium. Add tomatoes, jalapeños, chiles, beans, corn, and cashews; mix well. Reduce heat to low and simmer for at least 1 hour, stirring occasionally. Add salt and pepper. This is even better the next day!

Curried Potato, Apple, and Kale Soup

Makes 4–6 servings

The sweetness of the apples balances the bitterness of the kale, and the potatoes make the whole soup creamy and comforting.

> 1 large white onion, diced
> 2 pounds Yukon gold or russet potatoes, peeled and diced
>   (about 8 cups)
> 2 tablespoons canola oil
> 2 Golden Delicious apples, peeled and diced
> 1 large bunch kale, stems removed and diced (about 8 cups)
> 4 cups Vegetable Broth (page 10)
> 1 tablespoon cayenne pepper sauce
> 1 tablespoon curry powder
> Salt and pepper, to taste
> 1 tablespoon apple cider vinegar

Sauté the onion and potato in oil in a large stockpot over medium-high heat for about 5 minutes, until softened. Add in apples and sauté another 3–5 minutes, until softened. Add in all remaining ingredients except vinegar. Simmer slowly for 20 minutes.

Blend half of soup mixture in food processor or blender until smooth. Add back into pot. Remove from heat and stir in vinegar. Serve warm.

Showstopping Pumpkin Stew in a Pumpkin Centerpiece

Makes 6–8 servings

Perfect for Halloween, Thanksgiving, or any fall feast!

>1 medium pumpkin (8–10 pounds)
>Olive oil spray
>2 medium parsnips, peeled and chopped into bite-size pieces
>4 medium carrots, peeled and chopped into bite-size pieces
>4 medium russet potatoes, peeled and chopped into
>   bite-size pieces
>Salt and pepper, to taste
>6 to 8 Brussels sprouts, quartered and cores removed
>4 to 6 stalks celery with tops and chopped into bite-size pieces
>4 medium shallots, peeled and diced
>3 tablespoons olive oil
>3 cloves garlic, minced
>3 tablespoons flour
>4 cups Vegetable Broth (page 10)

Preheat oven to 425 degrees.

Cut top from pumpkin at a slant so that it will not fall through. Scrape all seeds and strings from inside pumpkin. Place pumpkin on a baking sheet and lightly spray inside and out with oil. Place top from pumpkin on baking sheet next to pumpkin. Bake for 30 minutes.

Spread parsnips, carrots, and potatoes on a baking sheet in a single layer and lightly spray with oil. Sprinkle with salt and pepper. Remove pumpkin from oven and place chopped vegetables in oven. Bake for 20 minutes. Remove vegetables from oven and toss in Brussels sprouts and celery and bake another 10–15 minutes, until all vegetables are tender and lightly browned.

Sauté shallots in oil over medium-high heat in a stockpot for about 2 minutes, until translucent. Add garlic and cook another minute or so, until fragrant. Stir in flour until absorbed. Stir in broth and all roasted vegetables and bring to a simmer. Pour mixture into pumpkin. Return filled pumpkin to baking sheet and bake with top on for 30 minutes.

Bring to the table and open top—steam will billow out and the smell will be amazing! Serve in small bowls. Scoop out some of the pumpkin flesh with a large spoon, so that each bowl has some large chunks of pumpkin.

Creamy Any Veggie Soup

Makes 6–8 servings

Endless possibilities abound with this simple soup because you choose the veggies!

>   1 cup diced onion
>   1 tablespoon olive oil
>   4 cups Vegetable Broth (page 10)
>   1½ pounds vegetables such as asparagus, broccoli, spinach,
>   bell peppers, or any combination, chopped (about 8 cups)
>   16 ounces silken tofu
>   1 tablespoon vinegar, of choice
>   Salt and pepper, to taste

In a large stockpot, sauté onion in oil over medium-high heat until translucent, 2–3 minutes. Add broth and vegetables and bring to a boil. Cover and reduce heat to a simmer and cook until vegetables are softened. (Firm vegetables take at least 20 minutes to soften.)

Purée the soup mixture with a stick blender or regular blender in batches. Add tofu and vinegar and blend until smooth. Add salt and pepper.

Note: Root vegetables such as sweet potatoes and hard winter squash such as butternut can be used in this soup, but should be roasted in the oven first until nearly cooked through.

Quatro Gazpachos

Makes 4 servings

The classic Spanish cold soup (it's a classic for good reason)—and three variations that will make you a gazpacho gourmet.

TRADITIONAL GAZPACHO

6 cups tomato juice, divided
2 ripe tomatoes, cored and quartered
1 medium onion, quartered
1 red bell pepper, cored and quartered (seeds and ribs removed)
½ cup cilantro
2 cloves garlic, chopped
Juice and zest of 1 lime
Cayenne pepper sauce, to taste
⅓ cup red wine vinegar
¼ cup extra virgin olive oil
1½ teaspoons salt
Freshly ground pepper, to taste

Combine 2 cups tomato juice in a food processor or blender with all the vegetables and the cilantro until smooth. Pour contents into a large bowl, add remaining juice, and thoroughly stir in the remaining ingredients. Chill for at least 2–3 hours before serving.

Garnish with any combination of the following: additional cilantro, scallions, diced avocado, chives, additional diced tomatoes or halved grape tomatoes, finely diced cucumber, and bell pepper.

WATERMELON GAZPACHO

Add 8 cups seedless watermelon cubes. Decrease tomatoes from 2 to 1 and omit juice.

SOUTHWEST AVOCADO GAZPACHO

Add 1 avocado and 1 jalapeño or Serrano pepper, and 1 can (4 ounces) tomato paste.

Add 2 large English cucumbers, peeled, cut in half, and seeded. Cut tomatoes and bell pepper in half lengthwise. Toss vegetables with a little olive oil. Grill over very high heat (about 450 degrees) until grill marks appear. Remove from grill and plunge into cold water to prevent veggies from cooking further.

Butternut Squash Bisque

Makes 6–8 servings

This soup manages to be both elegant and hearty, with a crispy shallot garnish, and is as suitable for a formal dinner party as it is for a cozy winter evening at home.

> 1 medium butternut squash, peeled, seeded, and cut in
>   chunks (about 3 cups)
> 3 tablespoons coconut oil
> 2 large shallots, minced (approximately ½ cup)
> 3 tablespoons flour
> ¼ cup dry sherry
> 1 can (14 ounces) regular coconut milk
> 4 cups Vegetable Broth (page 10)
> 1 teaspoon dried rosemary, crushed
> ½ teaspoon dried thyme
> 2 teaspoons salt
> ⅛ teaspoon nutmeg
> 1 bay leaf
> 1 tablespoon apple cider vinegar
> Freshly ground pepper, to taste

Preheat oven to 425 degrees. Line a baking sheet with parchment paper.

Place squash on prepared baking sheet and roast for 35–40 minutes, until squash is tender and cooked through. While squash is cooking, heat coconut oil over medium-high heat in a large stockpot then add shallots and sauté for 2–3 minutes, until they start to turn golden. Add flour and cook for 4–5 minutes, whisking continuously, until mixtures starts to turn a light golden blonde. Add sherry and stir up any remaining bits of roux and shallot that may have stuck to the bottom of the pot.

Add in coconut milk, broth, herbs, salt, nutmeg, and bay leaf, bringing mixture to just under a boil. Reduce heat to low and let simmer for 45 minutes, adding squash whenever roasting time is complete.

Using a stick blender or blending by batches in a regular blender, purée soup until desired texture and thickness is achieved. Finish with vinegar and top each bowl with pepper.

CRISPY SHALLOT GARNISH

Cut 2 large shallots across diameter to form ⅛-inch thick rings. Separate rings and toss in a little flour. Heat ½ inch canola or peanut oil in a small skillet to medium-high heat. Cook coated shallot rings in small batches so as not to crowd skillet. Cook until lightly browned and then drain on paper towels.

Creamy Tomato Basil Soup

Makes 6–8 servings

You won't miss the dairy in a mug of this hearty, healthy comforting classic.

1 large yellow onion, diced
2 tablespoons olive oil
4 cloves garlic, minced
1 cup minced fresh basil leaves
2 cans (28 ounces each) crushed tomatoes in purée
2 cups Vegetable Broth (page 10)
1 can (16 ounces) coconut milk
Salt and freshly ground pepper, to taste

In a large stockpot, sauté onion in oil over medium-high heat until translucent. Add garlic and sauté another 2–3 minutes. Add basil, tomatoes, and broth. Whisk in coconut milk then reduce heat and simmer for 20–30 minutes, stirring frequently. If a smoother consistency is desired, transfer to blender or food processor in batches or use a stick blender directly in the pot. Add salt and pepper and serve.

Caribbean Vacation in a Bowl

Makes 8–10 servings

Let your taste buds take a tropical vacation with this flavorful bowl of goodness.

1 large sweet potato (about 1 pound)

1 large yellow onion, diced

3 tablespoons olive oil

2 stalks celery, diced

4 cloves garlic, minced

2 tablespoons curry powder

¼ teaspoon allspice

1 teaspoon dried thyme leaves

1 Serrano chile, seeds and pulp removed and minced

4 cups Vegetable Broth (page 10)

1 cup long-grain rice, uncooked

1 can (14 ounces) coconut milk

1 large ripe mango, diced

5 or 6 green onions, thinly sliced

Cayenne pepper sauce, to taste

Salt and pepper, to taste

Preheat oven to 350 degrees.

Cut sweet potato in half lengthwise and place cut-side down on an oiled baking sheet. Bake for 40–50 minutes, until fork tender but not mushy. Remove from oven and let cool.

Cook onion in oil in a large stockpot over medium heat for about 3 minutes, until softened. Add in celery and garlic and cook another 3 minutes. Stir in curry powder, allspice, thyme, and chile and cook another minute.

Pour in broth and rice and bring to a boil. Reduce to a slow simmer, cover, and cook for about 20 minutes, until rice is tender. Cut sweet potato into ½-inch cubes and add to soup. Add in all remaining ingredients and cook just a few minutes, until heated through. Serve steaming hot.

Roasted Root Veggie Stew

Makes 4–6 servings

This rich and hearty stew is perfect for beating the fall or winter chill—so flavorful and comforting!

> 8 cups (2-inch) cubes root vegetables, such as beets, carrots, parsnips, or potatoes in any combination you like
> 4 tablespoons olive oil, divided
> Salt and pepper, to taste
> 4 cloves garlic, cut in half
> 1 large shallot, minced
> 1 tablespoon flour
> 6 cups Vegetable Broth (page 10)
> 2 tablespoons tomato paste
> 2 tablespoons red wine vinegar
> 1 cup dried lentils
> ½ cup diced parsley leaves

Preheat oven to 400 degrees.

Toss vegetable cubes with 2 tablespoons oil and spread on a baking sheet in a single layer. Sprinkle with salt and pepper. Roast for 35–40 minutes, until lightly browned and fork tender. Add garlic to baking sheet during the last 10 minutes.

While vegetables are roasting, in a large stockpot, sauté shallots over medium-high heat in remaining oil for 1 minute. Add in flour and cook another minute, stirring constantly.

Add the broth, tomato paste, vinegar, and lentils. Turn up heat to high and bring to a boil. Reduce to a simmer, cover, and cook about 20 minutes, until lentils are softened. Stir in roasted vegetables and parsley and serve piping hot.

Enlightened French Onion Soup

Makes 4–6 servings

Who says the French classic soup can't be just as delicious when meatless?

> 4 large yellow onions
> 4 tablespoons olive oil, divided
> 1 tablespoon dark brown sugar
> 1 teaspoon kosher salt
> 2 tablespoons flour
> 2 tablespoons red wine vinegar
> 2 bay leaves
> 4 cups Vegetable Broth* (page 10)
> 2 tablespoons lemon juice
> 2 tablespoons tomato paste
> 1 tablespoon thyme leaves
> 6 slices nondairy French bread

Slice onions from pole to pole in long strips about ¼ inch wide. Place in a large stockpot or Dutch oven with 3 tablespoons oil, brown sugar, and salt. Cover and cook over low heat, stirring every 10 minutes or so, until onions are soft and well browned, about 30–40 minutes.

Stir in flour and cook 5 minutes or so. Add in vinegar and turn heat to high, scraping up all bits from bottom of pan. Add in bay leaves, broth, lemon juice, tomato paste, and thyme and reduce to a simmer. Cover and cook another 10 minutes.

Brush both sides of bread slices with remaining oil. Broil for a few minutes 6 inches from heat until browned. Turn bread slices over and broil other side until browned. Serve soup in bowls with bread slices on top as a garnish.

* Use the variation of the broth with soy sauce for a darker, more robust broth.

Mama's Minestrone

Makes 4–6 servings

Old-world minestrone just like Mama always made, only better!

> 2 cups (½-inch) slices peeled carrots
> 2 tablespoons olive oil
> 2 stalks celery, cut in ½-inch slices
> 1 medium onion, cut in ½-inch pieces
> 2 cloves garlic, minced
> 2 cups chopped cabbage
> 2 cups (½-inch) slices zucchini
> 6 cups water
> 2 cups Vegetable Broth (page 10)
> 1 can (15 ounces) cannellini beans, drained
> 2 tablespoons balsamic vinegar
> 1½ cups vegetable juice or tomato juice
> ¼ cup diced parsley
> Salt and pepper, to taste

Sauté carrots in oil in a large Dutch oven or heavy-bottomed stockpot over medium-high heat for 2 minutes. Add celery and sauté another 2 minutes. Add onion and sauté another 2 minutes. Add garlic and cabbage and sauté another 2 minutes. Add zucchini and sauté another 2 minutes. Remove vegetables from pot and set aside to cool.

Add water and broth to pot and bring to a boil, scraping browned bits from bottom. Add beans and vinegar, reduce to a simmer and cover and cook for 30 minutes.

Return cooked vegetables to the pot then add in juice and parsley. Add salt and pepper. Serve immediately.

Potato Corn Chowder

Makes 6–8 servings

The New England perennial—without the clams. We think you'll love a mug of this on a cozy, cloudy afternoon.

2 tablespoons olive oil
1 onion, diced
1 stalk celery, diced,
1 large carrot, diced
2 tablespoons flour
2 large potatoes, cut into 1-inch cubes
4 cups Vegetable Broth (page 10)
1 can (14 ounces) coconut milk
2 cups corn
2 tablespoons apple cider vinegar
1 teaspoon liquid smoke
1 bay leaf
1 teaspoon thyme
2 teaspoons salt
½ teaspoon freshly ground pepper
Cayenne pepper sauce, to taste

In a large stockpot, heat oil over medium high. Add the onion, celery, and carrot and sauté for 5–6 minutes, until all vegetables are soft and just barely starting to brown. Stir in flour and cook for another 4–5 minutes, until well-incorporated and cooked through.

Add potatoes, broth, and coconut milk, and bring to a boil. Immediately reduce heat to low and add all remaining ingredients. Cover and simmer for at least 45 minutes, until potatoes are completely tender. Make sure to remove bay leaf before serving, and adjust seasoning, to taste.

Homestyle Hearty Lentil Soup

Makes 8–10 servings

This is a thick, nourishing classic, perfect for chilly evenings, and so satisfying that it serves as a meal in itself.

> 2 tablespoons coconut oil
> 1 large onion, diced
> 1 stalk celery, diced
> 1 large carrot, diced
> 2 cloves garlic, minced
> 1 can (14 ounces) diced tomatoes, with juice
> 6 cups Vegetable Broth (page 10)
> 2 cups brown or green lentils, rinsed and sorted
> 1½ teaspoons cumin
> 1 teaspoon coriander
> 1½ teaspoons salt
> ½ teaspoon freshly ground pepper
> 1 tablespoon balsamic vinegar
> ¼ cup packed fresh flat-leaf parsley, finely chopped

Heat oil over medium-high heat in a large, heavy stockpot. Add onion, celery, and carrot and sauté for about 5 minutes, until onions begin to soften. Add garlic and cook for another 2 minutes, stirring. Pour in tomatoes with juice, broth, lentils, cumin, coriander, salt and pepper.

Bring briefly to a boil, then reduce to low, cover, and simmer for 45 minutes. Lentils will be very tender. Taste for seasoning, and stir in vinegar. Using stick blender (or regular blender in small batches), purée until desired thickness and smoothness is reached. Garnish each bowl with chopped parsley.

Bountiful Borscht

Makes 10–12 servings

If you think of borscht as a cold magenta liquid, perhaps served with a single boiled potato, think again!

2 tablespoons coconut or olive oil
1 large onion, diced
1 stalk celery, diced
1 carrot, grated
1 green bell pepper, diced
2 to 3 cups cabbage, shredded (about ½ medium-size cabbage)
2 beets, grated
1 can (6 ounces) tomato paste
5 cloves garlic, minced
8 cups Vegetable Broth (page 10)
1 apple, diced
1 russet or Yukon gold potato, diced
1 bay leaf
1 tablespoon smoked paprika
Juice of 1 lemon
1 teaspoon salt
Freshly ground pepper, to taste
2 tablespoons fresh dill, minced, plus more for garnish,
   as desired

In a large stockpot, heat oil over medium high. Sauté onion, celery, carrot, and bell pepper until softened, 5–6 minutes. Add cabbage and beets and continue cooking, stirring occasionally, for another 10 minutes. Stir in tomato paste and garlic, incorporating fully, then add the broth, apple, potato, and bay leaf, raising heat to a boil. Reduce to simmer, cover, and cook for 20 minutes.

Add the paprika, lemon juice, salt, and pepper then cover again and cook over as low a heat as you can manage for at least another hour; 2 if possible. Serve with a generous sprinkling of fresh dill.

Cilantro Pesto Tortilla Soup

Makes 10–12 servings

This is a flavorful version of the classic southwest soup—with the freshness of raw veggies added before serving, and a flavor burst from a cilantro pesto garnish.

4 tablespoons vegetable oil, divided
2 cloves garlic, minced
1 tablespoon regular or chipotle chile powder
2 teaspoons cumin
1 tablespoon tomato paste
1 can (15 ounces) diced tomatoes with juice
8 cups Vegetable Broth (page 10)
Juice of 2 limes
2 large flour tortillas, cut into ¼-inch strips
½ cup diced cilantro leaves
¼ cup pine nuts or diced almonds
1 avocado, diced and tossed in lemon juice
3 green onions, thinly sliced

Preheat oven to 400 degrees.

Heat 1 tablespoon oil in a large stockpot over medium-high heat. Add garlic, chile powder, and cumin and cook about a minute, until very fragrant. Stir in tomato paste and tomatoes with juice. Add in broth and bring to a boil. Reduce heat and simmer for about 20 minutes. Stir in lime juice.

Meanwhile, spread tortilla strips in a single layer on a baking sheet, lightly spray with oil, and bake for 3–5 minutes, until lightly browned. In a food processor, process cilantro, nuts, remaining oil.

Ladle soup into bowls and garnish with a swirl of cilantro pesto, avocado chunks, green onions, and tortilla strips.

Toasted Hazelnut, Parsnip, and Leek Soup

Makes 6–8 servings

This was inspired by *Tangled;* the favorite movie of the moment for Anne's daughter (and Donna's granddaughter). A character made mention of a special hazelnut soup, so Anne set out to find a way to make one; we think you'll love the flavors!

1 cup raw hazelnuts, divided
2 cups plain, unsweetened almond milk, divided
2 tablespoons olive oil
½ yellow onion, diced
2 leeks, cut lengthwise then sliced into ½-inch pieces and
    rinsed well
3 large parsnips, peeled and grated
4 cups Vegetable Broth (page 10)
½ cup packed flat-leaf parsley, finely chopped, divided
1 teaspoon salt
½ teaspoon freshly ground pepper, plus more to finish
1 tablespoon apple cider vinegar

Soak half the hazelnuts overnight. Drain and gently rub inside a clean dish towel to remove most of the skins. Place in high-speed blender or food processor, add 1 cup almond milk, and purée until as smooth as possible (add more milk as needed). Set aside.

In a large stockpot, heat the oil over medium high and sauté onion for 2–3 minutes, until softened. Add leeks and sauté together for another 2–3 minutes then add parsnips and sauté all together for another 5–6 minutes. Stir in the broth, hazelnut mixture, remaining almond milk, half of the parsley, salt, and pepper.

Bring to a boil then reduce to low. Blend soup to desired smooth texture. Simmer for 30 minutes. Adjust seasonings, as desired.

While soup is cooking, preheat oven to 350 degrees. Toast remaining hazelnuts on a baking sheet for about 10–15 minutes. Immediately wrap in a clean dishtowel and let sit for 5 minutes. Remove as much of the skin as you can by rolling the hazelnuts against each other inside the towel; roughly chop and set aside until ready to serve soup.

Stir in vinegar just prior to serving. Sprinkle a little of the remaining parsley and toasted hazelnuts on each bowl, plus pepper, to taste.

Five-Minute Southwest Blender Chowder

Makes 6–8 servings

No, really—this hearty bowl of southwest bliss takes less than 5 minutes when using your blender, with corn tortillas providing the thickness!

1 plum tomato, core removed
1 medium carrot, peeled and chopped
½ red bell pepper, quartered
1 clove garlic
3 green onions, thinly sliced, divided
2 corn tortillas, torn in pieces
2 cups hot Vegetable Broth (page 10)
1 tablespoon lemon or lime juice
1 tablespoon soy sauce
1 teaspoon chipotle or regular chile powder
1 can (15 ounces) black beans, drained and divided
1 cup corn kernels, divided
Crushed tortilla chips, if desired

Add to blender, the tomato, carrot, bell pepper, garlic, a third of green onions, corn tortillas, broth, lemon juice, soy sauce, and chile powder. Blend until liquefied, about 1–2 minutes.

Add half of beans and half of corn. Pulse your blender a few times until beans and corn are in very small pieces. Stir in rest of beans and corn, and remaining green onions.

Serve warm, or if desired, heat each bowl in microwave for a steaming hot soup. Garnish with tortilla chips, if desired.

LUNCHES AND LIGHT FARE

Beet Tartare
Makes 4 servings

You'll do a double take when you first see this show-stopping dish. It has the look of classic tartare, but the light, fresh, sweet taste of roasted beets.

> 2 pounds beets
> 2 teaspoons lemon juice
> 1½ tablespoons cornstarch
> ¼ teaspoon each salt and pepper
> Canola oil spray
> 1 cup baby greens
> 1 tablespoon vinaigrette, of choice

Preheat oven to 350 degrees. Prepare 4 small ramekins with nonstick cooking spray.

Trim beets of tops and excess roots. Wrap each beet in aluminum foil and bake for about 60 minutes, until fork tender. Let cool to room temperature.

Peel beets and dice into very uniform small cubes, about ¼ inch. Toss beet cubes with lemon juice and then cornstarch and salt and pepper. Spoon beet mixture into prepared ramekins, pressing down cubes until tightly packed. Microwave at high power for 3 minutes. Remove and let cool to room temperature. Run a knife around edges of ramekins and then unmold onto center of small serving plates. Toss greens with vinaigrette and then mound them on top of beet mixture.

Good Ole Summertime Rolls

Makes 12 rolls

Crunchy fresh veggies wrapped in rice paper—a perfect light lunch!

1 red bell pepper, seeds and pulp removed
2 medium zucchini
3 carrots, peeled
¼ cup rice vinegar
1 tablespoon grated fresh ginger
2 cloves garlic, minced
1 tablespoon sugar
½ teaspoon kosher salt
¼ teaspoon pepper
2 cups thinly sliced bok choy (or cabbage)
½ cup diced cilantro
12 dried rice paper wrappers
Sweet and Spicy Asian Dipping Sauce (page 12)

Cut the bell pepper, zucchini, and carrots into matchsticks. Blanch, steam, or microwave until they are slightly softened and crisp-tender. Plunge into cold water.

Mix together the rice vinegar, ginger, garlic, sugar, salt, and pepper. Place this liquid in a large ziplock baggie with matchstick vegetables. Marinate 4–8 hours in refrigerator. Drain and combine vegetables with bok choy and cilantro.

Dip 1 sheet rice paper wrapper at a time into warm water for about 10 seconds and then lay flat on a cutting board. (Wrapper will continue to soften.) Place ½ cup of vegetable mixture on top and roll up as you would a burrito (fold sides over top of filling and then roll from side closest to you). Serve immediately with dipping sauce.

Chipotle Almond Sauce Nachos

Makes 6–8 servings

Who needs cheese when you can make this luscious spicy sauce in no time?

1½ cups unsweetened almond milk
Juice and zest of 1 lime
1 cup almond butter
1 teaspoon chipotle chile powder
1 teaspoon cumin
½ teaspoon salt
½ teaspoon cayenne pepper sauce
1 red bell pepper
1 poblano chile pepper
Canola oil spray
1 can (14 ounces) black beans, drained and rinsed
½ cup fresh or frozen and thawed corn
3 green onions, thinly sliced
12 cups tortilla chips, of choice

Place milk, lime juice, lime zest, almond butter, and spices in a blender in the order listed. Blend until very smooth. Taste and adjust seasonings, if desired.

Cut peppers into strips and spread on a baking sheet, skin sides up. Lightly spray with oil. Broil on highest setting in oven, about 6 inches from heat for 8–10 minutes, checking frequently so as not to burn. Remove from oven when skins begin to blacken. Let peppers cool slightly and then chop into bite-size pieces.

Pour almond sauce into a glass bowl and microwave for 60 seconds. Stir sauce and microwave again for 30 seconds.

Spread chips on a large platter. Drizzle heated almond sauce on top. Scatter black beans, corn, green onions, and chopped peppers on top. Serve immediately.

Dueling Garbanzos: Hummus Three Ways

Each recipe makes 3 cups

Hummus is a naturally vegan, endlessly adaptable, and highly nutritious food! If you've never made your own before, these are three great ways to get started.

ROASTED GARLIC HUMMUS

1 whole bulb garlic
3 tablespoons extra virgin olive oil, divided
2 teaspoons kosher salt, divided
1 tablespoon lemon juice
2 cans (15 ounces each) garbanzo beans, drained
1 teaspoon regular or smoked paprika
Cayenne pepper sauce, to taste
Water, as needed

Preheat oven to 350 degrees.

Cut the bulb of garlic in half across diameter. Place cut side up in a square of aluminum foil. Drizzle a little of the oil and salt on top. Wrap the aluminum foil around the bulb halves. Bake for 30 minutes.

Remove from oven, bring to room temperature, and then squeeze the cloves out of the bulb into the food processor. Process for a few pulses with all remaining ingredients except water. Turn food processor on and slowly add water in a thin stream until desired consistency.

SUN-DRIED TOMATO HUMMUS

3 cloves garlic, peeled
2 cans (15 ounces each) garbanzo beans, drained
Juice of ½ lemon
¼ cup tahini
¼ cup sun-dried tomatoes in oil, undrained
2 to 3 tablespoons rice or white vinegar
¼ cup extra virgin olive oil
½ teaspoon cumin
Salt, to taste

Place garlic in food processor and pulse to chop. Add garbanzo beans, lemon juice, tahini, tomatoes, and vinegar and pulse until very well mixed and starting to smooth out. Run the processor continuously as you drizzle in the oil. Continue running until it meets desired smoothness, occasionally scraping down the sides. Add the cumin and then salt, if needed.

HOT PINK HUMMUS

4 cloves garlic, peeled

1 medium beet, peeled and coarsely chopped

2 cans (15 ounces each) garbanzo beans, drained

Juice and zest of 1 lemon

⅓ cup extra virgin olive oil

¼ cup tahini

2 tablespoons rice vinegar

1 teaspoon cumin

½ teaspoon cinnamon

½ teaspoon salt

Place garlic in food processor and pulse to chop. Add all remaining ingredients and purée until smooth, adding more liquid if needed (either lemon juice or vinegar).

Note: For all three recipes, you may use dried garbanzo beans that have been soaked overnight then cooked until tender; approximately 45 minutes to an hour.

Bacon-less Wilted Spinach Salad

Makes 4–6 servings

Bacon, schmacon! This flavor-packed version will be your new favorite wilted spinach salad.

½ red onion
2 tablespoons canola oil
2 teaspoons sesame oil
1 teaspoon Dijon mustard
2 tablespoons rice vinegar
1 tablespoon agave nectar, stevia, sugar, or other sweetener
1 teaspoon salt
8 cups stemmed and chopped fresh spinach
½ cup sliced toasted almonds
1 tablespoon toasted sesame seeds
Eggplant Bacon (page 14) crumbled, optional

Cut onion into paper-thin slices about 2 inches long. Let onions soak in ice water while preparing rest of dish. Heat oils in a small saucepan to high heat. Mix together the mustard, vinegar, sweetener, and salt and add to pan. Heat to a boil.

Place spinach into a large serving bowl and then pour on hot mixture from pan. Immediately toss spinach until all leaves are coated.

Serve about 1 cup of salad on each plate and sprinkle with onions, almonds, and sesame seeds. Garnish with Eggplant Bacon, if desired. Serve immediately.

California Rainbow Chard Roll-Ups

Makes 6–8 rolls

This is a fabulously flavorful salad wrap that's perfect for summer—as pretty to serve as it is satisfying to eat!

 2 cans (15 ounces each) garbanzo beans, drained
 3 cloves garlic, minced
 1 avocado, peeled and pitted, divided
 2 to 3 tablespoons coconut oil
 Juice and zest of 1 lemon, divided
 1 teaspoon salt
 2 to 3 tablespoons rice vinegar
 1 bunch rainbow or red chard, rinsed and patted dry, excess
    stems removed
 1 cup alfalfa sprouts, or sprouts of choice
 1 large carrot, peeled and grated
 1 jar (8 ounces) marinated artichoke hearts
 ½ cup toasted pine nuts

Place garbanzo beans, garlic, half the avocado, coconut oil, half the lemon juice and all the zest, salt, and rice vinegar into a food processor and process until smooth—if you need more liquid, add a bit more vinegar. You could also add in a little bit of extra virgin olive oil.

Cut the remaining avocado half into slices. Spread out 1 chard leaf at a time, duller side up. Spread the leaf with about ¼ to ⅓ cup garbanzo mixture, depending on the size of the leaf. Add a layer of sprouts, then carrot, then a few artichoke hearts, and an avocado slice. Top with a squeeze of the remaining lemon half and a spoonful of toasted pine nuts. Roll up tightly and enjoy!

Roasted Garlic Ratatouille Rafts

Makes 8 servings

This easy, fun rendition of the classic Provençal dish is terrific as either a side dish or an appetizer, especially at the height of zucchini season.

4 large zucchini, halved lengthwise
2 tablespoons olive oil, plus extra for
    drizzling
½ teaspoon salt, plus more for
    sprinkling
1 bulb garlic
1 large onion, diced
1 medium eggplant, peeled and cubed into ½-inch pieces
1 red bell pepper, diced
½ cup sun-dried tomatoes, chopped (and drained of any oil,
    if packaged in oil)
Salt and freshly ground pepper, to taste
1 or 2 teaspoons balsamic vinegar
8 large leaves fresh basil, rolled and cut into thin ribbons

Preheat oven to 425 degrees. Lightly coat a baking sheet with olive oil. Scoop out the seedy center of each zucchini half and drizzle with a touch of olive oil. Sprinkle with salt and place cut-side down on baking sheet. Remove the excess papery skin off of the garlic bulb then cut off the top of the bulb so most of the cloves are exposed. Drizzle with olive oil, add a sprinkle of salt, and then wrap the bulb in foil.

Roast zucchini and garlic together, removing zucchini after about 15–20 minutes, once edges have browned and flesh is tender; continue roasting garlic for another 20 minutes, until cloves are very soft.

While zucchini and garlic are in the oven, heat 2 tablespoons olive oil in a large skillet over medium-high heat. Add onion and sauté for about 1–2 minutes, just until coated and starting to slightly soften. Add eggplant and sauté together with the onion, stirring frequently, for another 5 minutes. Add bell pepper and tomatoes and cook until all vegetables are cooked through. Season with salt and pepper.

Once garlic is done, squeeze softened cloves into a small bowl and mash with a fork. Add balsamic vinegar to the garlic and mix thoroughly until smooth; stir into eggplant mixture. Spoon filling into zucchini halves then top with the basil. Serve warm; a few minutes under a broiler to reheat just before serving will suffice if they've cooled down.

Roasted Beet and Hazelnut Salad

Makes 4 servings

This is a magical mix of flavors and textures—orange and thyme with the sweet beets and earthy hazelnuts. A perfect salad!

1½ pounds beets, peeled and cut into 1-inch cubes
1 teaspoon olive oil
Salt and pepper, to taste
2 tablespoons red wine vinegar
¼ cup frozen orange juice concentrate, thawed
1 tablespoon fresh thyme leaves
½ cup diced toasted hazelnuts

Preheat oven to 425 degrees.

Place beet cubes in a foil packet, drizzle with oil, and sprinkle lightly with salt and pepper. Seal in foil. Bake for 40–50 minutes, until beets are fork tender.

Toss beet cubes in a bowl with remaining ingredients and then let cool to room temperature before serving.

Crispy Tofu Cubes with Mango and Avocado

Makes 4 servings

This cold salad is refreshing and delightful with every sweet and sour bite!

½ cup sweet chile sauce
2 tablespoons rice vinegar
1 tablespoon grated fresh ginger
1 tablespoon soy sauce
16 ounces extra-firm tofu
2 tablespoons cornstarch
2 tablespoons canola oil
1 large ripe mango, peeled and diced
2 ripe avocados, peeled and diced
4 large lettuce leaves, torn into bite-size pieces

Stir together the chili sauce, vinegar, ginger, and soy sauce and set aside. Wrap tofu block with a kitchen towel and set between 2 dinner plates. Place a large can on top to press liquid from tofu. Let stand 20 minutes or so.

Cut pressed tofu into ½-inch cubes. Toss in cornstarch until evenly coated. Heat oil over medium-high heat in a large skillet. Cook tofu in 2 batches so as not to crowd pan. Turn occasionally until cubes are lightly browned on all sides. Remove to paper towels and pat off excess oil.

Toss together sauce, tofu cubes, mango, and avocado. Spread lettuce leaves on a salad plate. Mound the tofu mixture on top of lettuce leaves and serve immediately.

Fabulous Falafel

Makes 4–6 servings

These fabulous nuggets are soft on the inside and crunchy on the outside and perfect for topping a salad or tucking into a pita.

1 tablespoon flax seed meal
1 can (15 ounces) garbanzo beans, drained and rinsed
1 clove garlic, sliced
2 green onions, thinly sliced
1 tablespoon lemon juice
1 teaspoon cayenne pepper sauce
¼ cup diced parsley
2 teaspoons cumin
1 teaspoon coriander
1 teaspoon salt
¼ teaspoon baking soda
1 cup garbanzo bean flour or all-purpose flour, divided
½ tablespoon baking powder
Peanut or canola oil

Soak flax in 3 tablespoons hot water for about 5 minutes, until water is absorbed and mixture is sticky. Place flax mixture, garbanzo beans, garlic, onions, lemon juice, cayenne pepper sauce, and parsley in food processor and pulse until all ingredients are very small bits.

Whisk together cumin, coriander, salt, baking soda, ¾ cup flour, and baking powder. Stir this mixture into the garbanzo bean mixture. Form into patties using 2 tablespoons mixture. Chill in refrigerator for 30 minutes or up to 8 hours.

Heat ½ inch oil in a small skillet to about 350 degrees. Spread remaining flour on a small plate. Press patties into flour and then cook in small batches in oil for 2–3 minutes on each side, until golden brown. Serve immediately over salad greens or in a pita.

Asian Veggie Pot Stickers

Makes 24 pot stickers

This tasty restaurant favorite is naturally delicious in vegan form!

3 cups finely shredded cabbage
1 teaspoon salt
14 ounces extra-firm tofu, frozen and thawed, then drained
      and crumbled
4 green onions, finely chopped
2 cloves garlic, minced
1 tablespoon grated fresh ginger
1½ tablespoons tamari or soy sauce
2 dozen wonton wrappers
2 tablespoons peanut oil, divided
1 cup water, divided

In a large colander, toss cabbage and salt and let sit for half an hour in a sink. Press the cabbage down to squeeze out any excess moisture then transfer to a large bowl. Combine with crumbled tofu, green onions, garlic, ginger, and tamari then cover and refrigerate for at least 1 hour.

When ready to fill, lay wonton wrappers out on a flat surface. Place 1 heaping tablespoon of filling in the center of the square and then moisten the outer edges with water. Fold the square in half to create a triangle.

When half the wrappers are filled, heat 1 tablespoon oil in a nonstick skillet with lid and place pot stickers in the pan in a single layer. Cook uncovered over medium-high heat about 5 minutes, until golden on the bottom. Turn the pot stickers over and add ½ cup water to the pan, reduce heat to its lowest setting, and cover. Cook for about 10 minutes, or until most of the water is absorbed.

Remove cover and increase heat back to medium high; cook an additional 4 minutes. Transfer finished pot stickers to paper towels and repeat the process until all the filling has been used.

Tofu Pad Thai

Makes 4–6 servings

Many a tofu lover's first experience with this high-protein ingredient is in this perennial Thai mainstay, made vegan with almost no tweaking at all!

12 ounces rice stick noodles
4 tablespoons peanut oil, divided
14 ounces extra-firm tofu, drained, pressed, and cut into
    ½-inch cubes
4 tablespoons soy sauce, divided
½ red bell pepper, julienned
2 cloves garlic, minced
6 scallions, finely chopped
2 tablespoons brown sugar
3 tablespoons seasoned rice vinegar
1 teaspoon chile sauce
½ cup roasted salted peanuts, coarsely chopped
½ cup bean sprouts
1 lime, squeezed
¼ cup chopped cilantro

Boil rice noodles according to directions on package. Drain and toss with 1 tablespoon oil. Set aside. Heat another tablespoon of oil in a large skillet over medium high; add tofu cubes and 2 tablespoons soy sauce and sauté for about 4 minutes, stirring frequently until light brown. Remove from pan and set aside.

Add remaining oil to pan. Sauté bell pepper, garlic, and scallions for 5 minutes. Add brown sugar, rice vinegar, remaining soy sauce, and chili sauce and cook for another 2 minutes, stirring occasionally. Add rice noodles and tofu back to pan and stir all ingredients together, cooking until noodles and tofu are combined and heated. Toss in peanuts and bean sprouts, drizzle with lime juice, and scatter cilantro on top.

Toasted Walnut, Kale, and Cranberry Salad

Makes 6 servings

Anne's good friend Kelley brings a similar salad to every single potluck she attends—and it's a hit every time!

4 tablespoons extra virgin olive oil, divided
1 large bunch kale, stemmed and roughly chopped
½ cup dried cranberries
1 cup walnuts
1 tablespoon maple syrup
Juice and zest of 1 lemon
1 teaspoon brown mustard
½ teaspoon salt
Dash cayenne pepper sauce, optional

Preheat oven to 375 degrees. While oven is heating, in a large mixing bowl, massage 2 tablespoons of the oil into the kale leaves. Toss in cranberries; set aside.

Toast walnuts on a baking sheet until golden and fragrant, about 10–12 minutes (start checking at about 8 minutes). Remove from heat and let cool then chop. While nuts are toasting and then cooling, whisk together the remaining ingredients.

Pour dressing over the kale and cranberries and thoroughly toss together. The salad may be set aside for several hours before serving (either refrigerated or at room temperature). Add the chopped walnuts right before serving and toss again.

The Ultimate Veggie Burger

Makes 6 burgers

Even meat lovers will swoon over the hearty taste of these flavorful burgers.

1 cup old-fashioned rolled oats
3 slices toasted multi-grain bread, torn into pieces
½ cup walnuts
1½ cups cooked brown lentils
½ cup cooked black beans
1 tablespoon Balsamic vinegar
1 tablespoon soy sauce
2 teaspoons cumin
1 teaspoon liquid smoke
½ teaspoon cayenne pepper sauce
4 ounces cremini mushrooms
Vegetable oil

Pulse the oats and bread in a food processor until small crumbs. Mixture should be 3 cups, so add more breadcrumbs, if necessary. Add remaining ingredients except vegetable oil to food processor and pulse until mixture begins to come together in a clump. Form into patties, a little less than ⅔ cup for each patty. Refrigerate for at least 30 minutes, or several hours.

Heat a skillet to medium heat. Add a thin layer of oil to skillet. Cook patties for 5–6 minutes on first side, or until well browned. Turn and cook another 4–5 minutes, until browned on other side. Serve immediately.

ENLIGHTENED ENTRÉES

Paella Primavera

Makes 10–12 servings

This paella isn't just regular paella minus the meat—it is truly a festival of flavor. Roasting this perfect combination of vegetables makes the difference.

6 cups Vegetable Broth (page 10)
¼ teaspoon crumbled saffron threads
⅓ cup olive oil
½ large onion, diced
4 cloves garlic, minced
3 cups Arborio rice
½ cup dry white wine
2 teaspoons smoked paprika
1 teaspoon each turmeric, cumin, and kosher salt
1 medium zucchini, cut into ¼-inch thick half-moon slices
2 red bell peppers, diced
1 small jalapeño, diced
6 artichoke hearts, quartered
6 large shiitake or baby bella mushrooms, coarsely chopped
½ cup green peas
8 green onions, thinly sliced
1 medium tomato, seeded and diced
2 cups coarsely chopped spinach leaves
2 tablespoons minced parsley
Roasted red bell pepper strips and asparagus spears, optional

Preheat oven to 450 degrees.

Heat broth in a saucepan to just under a boil, reduce to a simmer, and add saffron. Heat oil in a paella pan or large, heavy-bottomed or cast iron skillet to medium-high heat. Add onion and sauté for 2–3 minutes. Add garlic and cook for 2–3 more minutes, until it starts to soften.

Add rice and stir well until grains are coated with oil. Add wine and stir until absorbed. Add broth, a little at a time, and stir until each addition is absorbed. Continue until rice is cooked through but still firm. Add spices, using a bit more turmeric if a deeper yellow is desired. Add salt.

Layer zucchini, bell peppers, jalapeño, artichoke hearts, mushrooms, peas, green onions, and tomato over the top of the rice mixture (do not stir in). Roast for about 15 minutes, until vegetables have started to brown. Remove from oven, stir vegetables and rice together, adding spinach and parsley.

Return to stove top and cook over medium heat for just about 5 minutes to create the crunchy crust on the bottom (don't stir, just keep an eye on it). Let rest for 10–15 minutes. Garnish with red pepper strips and asparagus and serve from the paella pan or skillet, spooning sauce over each serving.

SPICY GARLIC FINISHING SAUCE FOR PAELLA

¼ cup finely chopped red bell pepper
1 small jalapeño, diced
½ teaspoon ground cumin
½ teaspoon kosher or sea salt
4 cloves garlic, minced
1½ teaspoons fresh thyme leaves or ¼ teaspoon dried
1 teaspoon died oregano
½ cup olive oil, divided
¼ cup minced parsley

Purée the peppers, cumin, salt, garlic, thyme, oregano, and half the oil and parsley. Stir in the remaining oil and parsley. Spoon over servings of paella.

Mushroom and Red Chile Tamales
Makes 15–18 tamales

Tamales go vegan in a delicious healthy twist on a south-of-the-border staple.

30 to 40 dried corn husks
½ cup vegetable shortening
½ cup coconut oil

3½ cups masa harina

2 teaspoons baking powder

1 teaspoon garlic powder

1 teaspoon salt

3 cups Vegetable Broth (page 10)

3 tablespoons olive oil

1 pound cremini mushrooms, sliced ¼-inch thick

2 tablespoons flour

1 can (14 ounces) red chile sauce or red enchilada sauce

Salt and pepper, to taste

Soak the corn husks in hot water for at least 30 minutes. Whip the shortening and coconut oil with a mixer on high speed until light and fluffy, about 5 minutes. Set aside.

Meanwhile, stir together the masa, baking powder, garlic powder, and salt. Stir in the broth until well mixed. Let stand while making filling.

In a large skillet over medium high, heat oil and sauté mushrooms until they are softened, lightly browned, and most of liquid has evaporated, about 5 minutes. Stir in flour until absorbed. Stir in red chile sauce. Taste and add salt and pepper.

Stir together the masa mixture and whipped oil.

Remove corn husks from water and pat dry with a kitchen towel. Using the back of a spoon, spread ⅓ cup masa mixture onto corn husks in a rectangle about 5 inches wide and 3½ inches tall, about 2 inches from bottom of husks. Spoon about 2 tablespoons of mushroom mixture on top of masa in the center. Roll masa around filling by bringing sides of corn husks together, making sure that masa mixture completely surrounds the mushroom mixture in the middle. Then fold corn husks up from the bottom, about 2 inches. Place tamales in a steamer basket and steam over boiling water for about 30 minutes, until masa is firm. Serve immediately.

Braised Cabbage Rolls

Makes 6–8 servings

Slow simmering in a flavorful broth gives these enlightened rolls a classic homey taste.

1 large shallot, diced
3 tablespoons olive oil, divided
6 cloves garlic, divided
4 cups Vegetable Broth (page 10), divided
½ cup lentils
1 cup long-grain white rice
4 tablespoons soy sauce, divided
1 teaspoon cumin
8 large savoy cabbage leaves
2 tablespoons apple cider vinegar
2 tablespoons dark brown sugar
2 red bell peppers
2 tablespoons balsamic vinegar
1 can (6 ounces) tomato paste

Sauté the shallot in 1 tablespoon oil in a medium sauce pan over medium heat until softened, about 5 minutes. Mince 3 cloves garlic, add to pan, and sauté for another minute. Add in 2 cups of broth and lentils and simmer for 5 minutes. Add rice, 2 tablespoons soy sauce, and cumin; lower heat, cover, and simmer for about 20 minutes, until all liquid is absorbed.

Steam or microwave cabbage leaves for about 2–3 minutes, until softened. Remove from heat and rinse leaves in cold water. Cut the tough stem out at bottom center of each leaf. Roll ½ cup of rice mixture in each blanched leaf, jelly-roll style, tucking sides in as you go. Place seam side down in a large skillet so that rolls are all in a single layer, completely filling skillet. Stir vinegar and brown sugar into remaining 2 cups broth and pour over rolls in pan so that they are almost covered, adding a little water, if necessary. Simmer for about 30 minutes until leaves are soft and most of liquid has evaporated.

Preheat oven to 450 degrees. Cut bell peppers into strips and place cut side down on a baking sheet. Bake at top of oven for about 10–12 minutes, until softened and browned. Add remaining 3 cloves garlic to baking sheet for the last 5 minutes.

Blend in blender the remaining oil, red pepper strips, garlic, remaining soy sauce, balsamic vinegar, and tomato paste until very smooth. Drizzle over top of rolls before serving.

Spicy Ground Tofu Tacos
Makes 12 tacos

If you love classic tacos, try this new, improved version—with a better taste and texture than old-school hamburger filling.

¼ cup low-sodium tamari or soy sauce
1 tablespoon creamy peanut butter
1 teaspoon each cumin, garlic powder, and chile powder
½ teaspoon cayenne pepper sauce
16 ounces frozen and thawed extra-firm tofu
1 tablespoon olive oil or canola oil
12 taco shells
Taco toppings, such as salsa, tomatoes, and lettuce

Preheat oven to 350 degrees. Mix together tamari, peanut butter, spices, and cayenne pepper sauce in a medium bowl and set aside.

Drain water from tofu block by wrapping it in a thin kitchen towel and wringing out all liquid. Unwrap tofu and crumble into small bits into mixing bowl and toss with sauce.

Spread oil on a baking sheet. Sprinkle crumbled tofu on top of oil in a thin layer. Bake for 20 minutes. Remove from oven and stir. Return to oven and cook for about 20 more minutes, until moisture is almost gone and tofu is crispy. Spoon mixture into taco shells and top with desired toppings.

Battle of the Bologneses!

Makes 4–6 servings

Diners will ask, "What meat did you use?" This incredible sauce has a rich, savory, and yes—"meaty" flavor without meat.

> ½ ounce dried porcini or shiitake mushrooms
> 2 tablespoons canola oil
> 1 large white or yellow onion, diced
> 2 stalks celery, diced
> 2 large carrots, peeled and diced
> 8 ounces cremini mushrooms, diced
> 3 cloves garlic, minced
> 2 tablespoons soy sauce
> 1 tablespoon balsamic vinegar
> 1 cup Vegetable Broth (page 10)
> 1 can (28 ounces) crushed tomatoes in purée
> Salt and pepper, to taste

Pulverize the dried mushrooms in a spice grinder or food processor to a fine powder and set aside.

Heat oil in a large Dutch oven to medium-high heat. Add onion, celery, and carrots and sauté 5 minutes, stirring frequently. Add in cremini mushrooms and garlic and sauté about another 5 minutes, until all vegetables are very soft. Add pulverized dried mushrooms, soy sauce, vinegar, broth, and tomatoes. Bring to a boil.

Reduce heat to low and simmer for 40–50 minutes, stirring occasionally, until sauce is very thick. Add salt and pepper. Serve with pasta.

ANNE'S LENTIL BOLOGN-EASY SAUCE

Makes 4–6 servings

A savory lentil version of a bolognese—packed with fiber and protein and all kinds of goodness.

½ cup red lentils, rinsed and sorted
2 tablespoons olive oil
1 onion, diced
4 cloves garlic, minced
1 can (6 ounces) tomato paste
1 tablespoon balsamic vinegar
2 tablespoons vegan Worcestershire sauce
1 can (14 ounces) diced tomatoes
2 teaspoons dried basil
1 teaspoon dried oregano
1 teaspoon smoked paprika
1 teaspoon salt
Freshly ground pepper, to taste
1 cup Vegetable Broth (page 10)
½ cup coconut milk, optional

Place lentils in a medium saucepan, cover with water, and boil for 15 minutes then drain and set aside. Heat oil in a large skillet, add onion, and cook until softened, about 3–4 minutes. Add garlic and cook another 2 minutes or so. Add tomato paste, mixing in well with the garlic and onions. Stir and scrape the bottom of the pan frequently so the tomato paste cooks and the onions brown a bit but not burn.

Add vinegar and Worcestershire sauce, stirring the browned bits off the bottom of the pan. Add diced tomatoes, spices, and broth. Bring the mixture to a boil. Add lentils back in and reduce to a low simmer for about 25 minutes, until liquids are reduced and mixture is thickened, stirring occasionally. Finish with coconut milk, if using, and adjust seasoning, to taste. Serve with your favorite pasta, rice, or quinoa.

All-American Meatless Loaf

Makes 1 loaf, serves 4–6 people

Yes, it's true, this classic 1950s retro dish is yummy meatless!

1 cup brown lentils
2 medium carrots, peeled
1 cup diced Medjool dates
1 medium onion, diced
1 stalk celery, diced
2 tablespoons olive oil
2 cloves garlic, minced
1 tablespoon cumin
2 tablespoons steak sauce, of choice
2 tablespoons soy sauce
1 cup multi-grain bread crumbs
½ cup ground or very finely minced pecans
1½ cups cooked rice
3 tablespoons flax seed meal, softened in ½ cup boiling water

Preheat oven to 350 degrees.

Cook lentils in boiling salted water for 30 minutes, or until very soft. Drain well. Place in food processor and pulse until very small bits.

Grate the carrots on the large holes of a box grater. Sauté the carrots, dates, onion, and celery in oil in a large skillet over medium-high heat for 6–8 minutes, until very soft, stirring frequently to remove moisture. Add in garlic, cumin, steak sauce, and soy sauce and cook another minute. Add this skillet mixture to food processor and pulse until very well blended. Empty mixture into a large bowl. Stir in breadcrumbs and then pecans, rice, and flax seed.

Place an aluminum foil sling into a loaf pan and prepare with cooking oil spray. Spoon mixture into pan, pressing mixture down so that no air pockets remain. Bake for 30 minutes at center of oven.

While loaf is baking, make a glaze by simmering 1 cup ketchup, ¼ cup brown sugar, and 1 tablespoon vinegar in a small saucepan for about 2 minutes, until thickened slightly. Remove loaf from oven and spread glaze on top. Return to oven and bake another 20 minutes.

Thai Sweet Potato Coconut Curry

Makes 4–6 servings

This is a great introduction to Thai-style curries, and packed with nutrition, too!

2 tablespoons coconut oil
1 large onion, thinly sliced
1 red bell pepper, julienned
4 cloves garlic, minced
3 tablespoons grated fresh ginger
2 cups Vegetable Broth (page 10)
1 can (14 ounces) coconut milk
1 large sweet potato, diced into ½-inch cubes
1 teaspoon green curry paste
½ teaspoon turmeric
½ teaspoon red pepper flakes
½ teaspoon salt
Juice and zest of 1 lime
¼ cup basil leaves, cut into thin ribbons

Heat oil over medium high in a large skillet. Add onion and bell pepper and sauté for about 6–8 minutes, until vegetables are slightly softened and lightly browned. Add garlic and ginger, and cook for another 3–4 minutes. Stir in broth, coconut milk, and sweet potato. Bring to a boil then reduce to simmer for 25–30 minutes, or until sweet potato is tender.

While simmering, stir in curry paste, turmeric, red pepper flakes, and salt. Finish with lime and basil, and adjust spices to taste. Serve over rice, quinoa, or all on its own.

Lentil Sloppy Joes

Makes 4 servings

Who doesn't love Sloppy Joes? This meatless version is packed with flavor with the same taste and comfort feel as the original American classic sloppy sandwich.

1½ cups brown lentils
1 red onion, diced
1 green bell pepper, diced
2 tablespoons canola oil
3 cloves garlic, pressed
1 can (6 ounces) tomato paste
4 tablespoons soy sauce
3 tablespoons balsamic vinegar
3 tablespoons brown sugar
1 tablespoon vegan Worcestershire sauce or steak sauce
1 teaspoon each smoked paprika and oregano
1 tablespoon cumin
1 tablespoon dried mustard
4 cups Vegetable Broth (page 10)
Salt and pepper, to taste

Bring a large pot of salted water to a boil. Add lentils and boil for 30 minutes. Turn off heat and let sit another 10 minutes. Drain and set aside.

In a large skillet over medium-high heat, sauté onion and bell pepper in oil until softened, about 3 minutes. Add in garlic and sauté another minute. Add lentils and remaining ingredients to skillet mixture. Bring to a simmer. Cover and simmer, stirring frequently, for about 30 minutes, until lentils are softened but still intact and almost all liquid has evaporated. Adjust salt and pepper, if needed. Serve over toasted buns of your choice.

Meatless Masala with Roasted Garbanzos

Makes 6–8 servings

This take on chana masala loses the heavy cream and adds an extra layer of flavor by roasting the garbanzo beans.

ROASTED GARBANZOS

1 can (14 ounces) garbanzo beans, drained and rinsed
2 tablespoons olive oil
1 teaspoon salt
½ teaspoon each cumin and coriander
¼ teaspoon each chile powder and garlic powder

If using dried garbanzo beans, soak at least 12 hours, rinse, and then boil for 1 hour. Drain and allow to cool and dry spread out on a large baking sheet. If using canned, rinse and spread out to dry the same way.

Preheat oven to 350 degrees. Drizzle garbanzos with olive oil. Mix the spices together and then sift evenly over the garbanzos, rolling gently with your hand. Place in oven and roast for about 45 minutes, shaking pan periodically. Make sauce while they're in the oven.

SAUCE

2 tablespoons coconut oil
½ large yellow onion, chopped
3 cloves garlic, minced
1 (1-inch) chunk fresh ginger, grated (about 1½ tablespoons)
1 can (28 ounces) crushed tomatoes (preferably fire-roasted)
1 can (14 ounces) coconut milk, divided
1½ teaspoons garam masala
½ teaspoon each chili powder, turmeric, and cumin
2 tablespoons maple syrup
2 to 3 tablespoons fresh lemon juice
1 teaspoon salt

Heat the coconut oil in a large skillet over medium high. Add onion and sauté for 4–5 minutes, until softened and beginning to brown. Add in garlic and ginger and cook for another 2–3 minutes. Pour the crushed tomatoes and all but ½ cup of the coconut milk into the pan, stir to combine. Add spices, maple syrup, and lemon juice, and adjust to taste (you may want to add more chile powder if you like it spicier). Lower heat and simmer for 30 minutes, reducing slightly.

Stir in the roasted garbanzos just before serving so they retain a little crispiness and swirl in the remaining coconut milk. Serve over rice, if desired.

Roasted Eggplant Bourguignon
Makes 6 servings

Eggplant and portobello mushrooms contribute a deep, earthy flavor to this update of the classic savory stew.

2 medium eggplants, halved lengthwise and sliced into
¼-inch pieces
5 tablespoons olive oil, divided
2 tablespoons each fresh thyme and rosemary, divided
4 Yukon gold potatoes, cubed
1 teaspoon salt
½ teaspoon freshly ground pepper
1 large onion, thinly sliced
1 carrot, sliced
1 stalk celery, sliced
2 cloves garlic, minced
1 can (6 ounces) tomato paste
1 cup burgundy or other deep, rich red wine
3 cups mushroom broth
10 to 12 ounces small brown button or baby bella
mushrooms, halved
3 tablespoons coconut oil, divided
16 ounces frozen pearl onions
1 tablespoon brown rice flour or other flour of choice

Preheat the oven to 425 degrees.

Toss eggplant slices in 2 tablespoons oil and 1 tablespoon each of the herbs. Do the same with the potatoes, tossing in 2 tablespoons oil plus remaining herbs; season all with salt and pepper. Place eggplant and potatoes on a baking sheet and roast; taking eggplant out after 15 minutes and continuing to roast the potatoes until they're golden on the outside and soft on the inside; another 15 minutes or so, giving the pan an occasional shake.

While the vegetables are roasting, heat the remaining tablespoon of oil in a large stockpot over medium-high heat. Add the onion and sauté for just a few minutes, until it starts to soften. Add the carrot and celery, cooking another 5–6 minutes. Add the garlic and sauté just until it becomes fragrant then add the tomato paste. Stir the paste in well, coating all the vegetables and also browning it a bit as you go.

Pour in the wine, stirring up the browned remnants at the bottom of the pot then add the mushroom broth. Bring it all up to a boil then add the mushrooms and reduce heat to a simmer. By now, the eggplant should be about ready; remove from the oven and add to the pot.

Cook on low for about 10 minutes as you prepare the pearl onions. Heat 2 tablespoons coconut oil in a small saucepan, add the onions, and sauté for about 5 minutes. Combine remaining coconut oil with the flour with a fork or your fingertips and stir into the main pot of stew. Transfer cooked onions to the stew. Now check the thickness of the liquid—if there's not enough liquid, add another cup of broth or so. Serve with the roasted potatoes.

Sautéed Greens on Pumpkin Polenta

Makes 4–6 servings

This rich and satisfying dish is the perfect blend of flavors and textures.

4 cups Vegetable Broth (page 10)
2 tablespoons vegan margarine
2 teaspoons smoked paprika
2 teaspoons cumin
1½ cups coarsely ground polenta
1 can (16 ounces) pumpkin
¼ cup nutritional yeast
Salt and pepper, to taste
8 cups chopped spinach, or greens of choice
1 tablespoon extra virgin olive oil
2 ounces pecans, chopped (½ cup)
½ cup diced sweetened dried cranberries
1 tablespoon apple cider vinegar

In a large saucepan, bring the broth, margarine, paprika, and polenta to a simmer and cook for about 20 minutes, stirring frequently until smooth and thick. Turn off heat and stir in pumpkin and nutritional yeast, adding salt and pepper.

In a small skillet, sauté greens in oil over medium-high heat until wilted, about 2 minutes. Stir in pecans, cranberries, and vinegar. Season with salt and pepper and remove from heat.

Serve by spreading polenta on a serving plate and then spoon on sautéed greens topping.

Mac and Cashew Cheese

Makes 6–8 servings

Classic cheese sauce has met its match with this rich and creamy version!

2 cups raw cashews
16 ounces macaroni
2 large carrots, peeled and sliced ¼-inch thick
3 tablespoons olive oil
1 large onion, diced
2 cloves garlic, minced
1 teaspoon salt
1½ cups Vegetable Broth (page 10)
3 tablespoons lemon juice
1 tablespoon cayenne pepper sauce
8 ounces silken tofu
½ cup coconut milk
¼ cup nutritional yeast
½ cup finely crushed potato chips

Cover cashews in boiling water and let soak at least 30 minutes. Cook macaroni in salted water to al dente stage according to package directions.

In a large skillet, sauté carrots in oil for 2 minutes over medium-high heat. Add onion and cook another 3 minutes. Add in garlic and cook another minute or so, until garlic is fragrant and all vegetables are softened.

Drain water off of cashews and place nuts in a blender with skillet mixture, salt, broth, lemon juice, and cayenne pepper sauce; blend until very smooth. Add tofu, coconut milk, and nutritional yeast and blend again until very smooth. Stir together the blender mixture and macaroni.

Spread in a 9 x 13-inch pan and sprinkle potato chips on top. Broil about 3–6 inches from heat until lightly browned. Serve immediately

Roasted Mushroom Medley Stroganoff

Makes 4–6 servings

Roasted mushrooms are perfect over rice or noodles in this hearty and flavorful version of the classic dish.

1 pound cremini mushrooms
8 ounces oyster mushrooms
8 ounces shiitake or maitake
    mushrooms
4 tablespoons olive oil, divided
2 yellow onions, cut in julienne strips
2 tablespoons flour
3 cups Vegetable Broth (page 10)
1 tablespoon red wine vinegar
3 tablespoons soy sauce
16 ounces silken tofu
1 tablespoon lemon juice
1 tablespoon Dijon mustard
1 tablespoon tomato paste
1 teaspoon dried thyme leaves
Salt and pepper, to taste
Cooked rice or noodles

Preheat oven to 425 degrees.

Slice mushrooms into ¼-inch slices and toss in 2 tablespoons of oil. Spread in a single layer on a baking sheet and bake at top of oven for about 8–10 minutes, until mushrooms are softened and lightly browned. Remove from oven and set aside.

Cook onion strips in remaining oil over medium heat in a large skillet until browned and softened, about 5 minutes. Stir in flour until absorbed, about 1 minute. Stir in broth, vinegar, and soy sauce and simmer for 8–10 minutes, stirring frequently until liquid is thickened and reduced by half.

Using a blender, blend the tofu, lemon juice, Dijon mustard, and tomato paste together until smooth.

Remove skillet from heat and stir in mushrooms, thyme, and salt and pepper. Stir in the tofu mixture. Serve immediately over rice or noodles.

Sublime Shepherd's Pie

Makes 4 servings

This classic comfort dish is a cinch to throw together, and you won't miss the meat, not even a tiny bit!

1 pound Yukon gold potatoes
2 tablespoons vegan margarine
½ cup unsweetened rice, soy, or almond milk
1 teaspoon salt
2 tablespoons olive oil
1 large onion, diced
1 cup diced carrot
¾ cup fresh or frozen and thawed corn
½ teaspoon dried thyme leaves
1 tablespoon soy sauce
2 tablespoons cornstarch
2 cups Vegetable Broth (page 10)
1½ cups cooked lentils

Preheat oven to 350 degrees.

Cut potatoes into 2-inch chunks and boil in salted water until fork tender. Mash potatoes with margarine, milk, and salt. Set aside.

Heat oil in a large skillet to medium-high heat. Sauté onion and carrots until softened, 4–5 minutes. Stir in corn, thyme, and soy sauce. Stir in cornstarch until absorbed. Stir in broth and bring to a simmer. Stir in lentils and then spoon skillet mixture into an 8 x 10-inch casserole dish. Top with mashed potatoes. Bake 25–30 minutes, until bubbly around edges.

Tuna-less Casserole

Makes 6–8 servings

The classic American casserole goes meatless—but with all the comforting flavor and texture as the original.

    12 ounces wide eggless noodles
    6 tablespoons extra virgin olive oil, divided
    1 large shallot, diced
    2 stalks celery, diced
    8 ounces cremini mushrooms, diced
    ½ teaspoon each salt and pepper
    ½ cup flour
    4 cups unsweetened rice or almond milk
    1 tablespoon lemon juice
    1 tablespoon soy sauce
    1 teaspoon cayenne pepper sauce
    ¼ cup nutritional yeast
    1 cup frozen diced carrots and peas, thawed
    1 cup finely crushed potato chips

Boil noodles in salted water to al dente stage. Drain.

Heat 2 tablespoons oil in a large skillet over medium-high heat. Add shallots and celery and cook about 3 minutes, until softened. Remove vegetables from skillet to a large bowl. Add mushrooms to skillet. Sprinkle with salt and pepper and sauté for about 3 minutes, until most of liquid has evaporated. Add mushrooms to bowl.

Add remaining oil to skillet. Whisk in flour and cook for about 2 minutes, stirring constantly. Whisk in milk and simmer until thickened. Stir in lemon juice, soy sauce, cayenne pepper sauce, and nutritional yeast. Stir in all cooked vegetables and peas and carrots. Stir in cooked noodles.

Spread mixture in an 8 x 10-inch baking pan. Sprinkle with potato chips and broil for a few minutes, until lightly browned. Serve immediately.

The Ultimate Veggie Pot Pie

Makes 6–8 servings

This is the classic American comfort dish taken to the limit—the perfect blend of veggies in a rich sauce topped with flaky puff pastry. Meet perfection in casserole form!

1 ounce dried porcini mushrooms
1 large russet potato, peeled
1 large carrot, peeled
1 stalk celery
6 tablespoons olive oil, divided
1 large shallot, diced
¼ cup flour
2 cups unsweetened soy, almond, or rice milk
1 cup frozen peas
½ teaspoon dried thyme leaves
Salt and pepper, to taste
1 sheet frozen puff pastry, thawed

Preheat oven to 400 degrees.

Soak mushrooms in 2 cups boiling water for 20 minutes. Drain and reserve ½ cup of soaking liquid. Dice mushrooms and set aside.

While mushrooms are soaking, cut potato and carrot into small cubes, a little bigger than ¼ inch. Cut celery in half lengthwise and then into ¼-inch slices. Heat a large skillet to medium-high heat. Add 2 tablespoons oil, shallot, potato, carrot, and celery and sauté for 3–5 minutes, until fork tender, stirring frequently. Remove vegetables from skillet.

Add remaining oil to skillet. Whisk in flour and cook for 1 minute. Whisk in milk and reserved mushroom water. Simmer until thickened, about 2 minutes. Add sautéed vegetables, mushrooms, peas, thyme leaves, and then salt and pepper. Pour skillet mixture into a 9 x 13-inch pan.

Pierce pastry about every ½ inch with a fork. Place pastry on top of casserole. Cut several large slits in top for steam to escape. Bake for 35–40 minutes, until bubbly and browned.

Creamy Green Chile Enchiladas

Serves 6–8

This is based on a family original, spanning three generations and counting, now rendered vegan—and every bit as delicious.

¼ cup coconut oil, or more as needed
12 corn tortillas
1 red bell pepper, diced
2 cups butternut squash, shredded
¼ cup olive oil plus 2 tablespoons, divided
1 bunch green onions, thinly sliced (reserve some for garnish)
1 can (14 ounces) black beans, rinsed and drained
2 teaspoons cumin
1 teaspoon chipotle chili powder
¼ cup flour
2 cups Vegetable Broth (page 10)
1 can (4 ounces) diced green chiles
1 can (16 ounces) regular coconut milk
Hot pepper sauce and salt, to taste
1 tomato, chopped

Preheat oven to 350 degrees. Melt the coconut oil in a medium skillet over medium heat. Soften tortillas by dipping in the oil for a few seconds on each side. Set aside to cool while you make the filling and sauce.

In the same skillet, sauté bell pepper and squash in 2 tablespoons olive oil for 4–5 minutes, until vegetables begin to soften. Do not overcook. Stir in onions, beans, and spices. Set aside and let cool while sauce is prepared.

Heat remaining olive oil in a large saucepan over medium high. Add the flour, whisking until well absorbed, but not browned. Add broth and chiles, bringing to a gentle boil. Whisk in coconut milk. Bring back to a boil just for a moment then reduce heat to low and simmer, whisking, until sauce starts to thicken. Add dash of hot pepper sauce and salt. Remove from heat.

Spread ½ cup of the sauce in the bottom of a 9 x 1-inch baking dish. Place about ⅓ cup of the squash mixture in the center of each tortilla and roll up tightly, enchilada style. Place rolls snugly, side-by-side, in the pan on top of the sauce. Pour remaining sauce evenly over the top. Bake for about 30–40 minutes, until bubbly. Garnish with a few sprinkles of green onions and tomato.

Spinach and Mushroom Korma

Serves 4–6

Korma is a cousin to curry—the same great creamy dish with different flavors.

1 tablespoon coarsely grated fresh ginger
1 small tomato, diced
1 teaspoon cumin
½ teaspoon coriander
1 teaspoon salt, divided
1 cup water
2 tablespoons vegetable oil
1 medium yellow onion, peeled and cut in ¼-inch strips
16 ounces cremini mushrooms, sliced ¼-inch thick
8 ounces baby spinach leaves
1 can (15 ounces) garbanzo beans, drained and rinsed
½ cup coconut milk
Salt and pepper, to taste
6 cups cooked rice

Combine the ginger, tomato, cumin, coriander, ½ teaspoon salt, and water in a blender and blend until smooth. Heat oil in a large skillet over medium high heat. Add the onion and sauté until lightly browned, about 5 minutes. Add the mushrooms and sauté for another 2–3 minutes, until vegetables are softened. Remove vegetables from pan.

Add the blender mixture to the pan and simmer until thickened, about 5 minutes. Stir in onion mixture, and simmer for a few minutes. Add in spinach and garbanzo beans, and simmer until heated through, 2–3 minutes. Stir in coconut milk and season with salt and pepper, as desired. Serve warm over rice.

Pineapple Fried Rice

Makes 6–8 servings

This meatless version of the classic Asian dish is full of contrasting flavors and textures, and is a fabulous way to use up leftover rice.

1 large sweet onion, such as Vidalia or Walla Walla
1 red bell pepper, stem and seeds removed
2 tablespoons peanut oil
1 teaspoon sesame oil
2 green onions, thinly sliced
3 cups cold cooked white or jasmine rice
3 cloves garlic, pressed
1 tablespoon grated fresh ginger
1 tablespoon rice vinegar
1 teaspoon chile garlic sauce
¼ cup low-sodium soy sauce
1½ cups diced pineapple
½ cup roasted cashew pieces
¼ cup diced cilantro

Cut onion and bell pepper into matchstick pieces about ¼-inch wide and 2 inches long.

Heat oils in a large skillet or wok to medium-high heat. Add in onion and sauté for 2 minutes, or until onion begins to soften. Add bell pepper and green onions and cook another minute. Remove vegetables from skillet, leaving as much oil in pan as possible.

Add rice to skillet, patting it down so that it is in a layer with as much rice touching the skillet bottom as possible. Let sit for about 3 minutes then start breaking up rice and turning it over in clumps with a spatula. Continue cooking and breaking up rice until parts of rice have a lightly browned and crispy texture.

Stir together the garlic, ginger, vinegar, chile sauce, and soy sauce and stir into skillet mixture. Stir in cooked onion and pepper mixture. Stir in pineapple, cashews, and cilantro until well distributed. Taste and add more of the vinegar, chile sauce, or soy sauce, as desired.

Veggie Samosa Pie

Makes 6–8 servings

Quick. Flavorful. Healthy. What more could you ask for in a main dish easy enough to make on a busy weeknight?

> 1 pound russet potatoes, peeled and cut in 2-inch chunks
> 2 tablespoons vegan margarine
> 2 tablespoons vegetable oil, divided
> 1 medium onion, diced (about 1 cup)
> 1 large carrot, peeled and diced (about ½ cup)
> 3 cloves garlic, pressed
> 1 tablespoon black or yellow mustard seeds
> 1 teaspoon each curry powder, coriander, and cumin
> 1 pinch red pepper flakes
> 1 cup frozen peas
> 1 cup Vegetable Broth (page 10)
> Salt and pepper, to taste
> 1 Perfect Pie Crust (page 15)
> Vegetable oil spray

Boil potatoes in salted water for 20 minutes, or until fork tender. Drain, return to pot, add margarine, and mash into chunks the size of grapes.

Preheat oven to 350 degrees.

Heat 1 tablespoon oil in skillet over medium-high heat. Add onion and carrot and sauté 5 minutes, or until carrot is tender. Scoot vegetables to the outside edge of skillet. Add remaining oil, garlic, mustard seeds, and all spices in center of skillet. Cook another minute or so until fragrant. Stir in peas and broth. Fold skillet mixture into potato mixture. Season with salt and pepper. Spoon mixture into a 9-inch pie pan. Set aside.

Roll out pastry and cut into an 11-inch circle on floured work surface. Cover filling with dough and crimp edges with fingers. Cut slits in pastry to allow steam to escape. Lightly spray with oil to help crust to brown.

Place pie on baking sheet and bake 45–50 minutes, or until crust is lightly browned. Serve warm.

Polenta Spinach Spirals

Makes 4–6 servings

Polenta rolled up with sautéed greens makes pretty spirals on your plates. And the flavors are a match made in heaven!

> 4 cups Vegetable Broth (page 10)
> 1½ cups yellow cornmeal
> 4 tablespoons extra virgin olive oil, divided
> ⅓ cup nutritional yeast
> 1 large onion, diced
> 3 cloves garlic, minced
> 2 boxes (10 ounces each) frozen chopped spinach, thawed and squeezed dry
> Dash of nutmeg
> 1 teaspoon cayenne pepper sauce
> Salt and pepper, to taste

Bring broth to a boil and slowly stir in cornmeal. Reduce heat and simmer for about 5 minutes, stirring frequently, until very thick. Remove from heat and stir in 2 tablespoons of oil and nutritional yeast.

Line an 11 x 17-inch baking pan with 2 layers of plastic wrap and then spray lightly with oil. Pour polenta onto baking sheet and spread evenly out, to about 1-inch thickness. Cool to room temperature.

Sauté onion in remaining oil for about 2 minutes over medium-high heat, until softened. Add garlic and cook another minute or so until fragrant. Add in spinach and sauté for a few more minutes, until all moisture is removed. Stir in nutmeg, cayenne pepper sauce, and salt and pepper.

Spread greens evenly on top of polenta. Carefully roll up polenta like you would a jelly roll, from the shortest side, using plastic wrap to help then removing it as you go. Chill until set.

Remove from refrigerator and slice into 2-inch thick pieces and place spiral sides up on a serving platter. Microwave for about 2 minutes, until heated through.

SENSATIONAL SIDES

Hazelnut Quinoa Stuffed Bell Peppers

Makes 6 servings

This retro recipe brings back comfort food memories and gets a delectable upgrade!

> 1 cup quinoa
> 2 cups water
> ½ teaspoon salt
> 3 large red or orange bell peppers
> 1 shallot, minced
> 2 tablespoons olive oil
> ½ cup diced hazelnuts
> 1 teaspoon cumin
> 2 cloves garlic, minced
> 2 cups chopped spinach leaves
> Cooking oil spray

Add quinoa, water, and salt to a small saucepan and bring to a boil. Cover and reduce to a simmer. Simmer for 15 minutes and remove from heat and let stand.

Preheat oven to 350 degrees.

Cut bell peppers in half lengthwise and scoop out seeds and pulp. Place in an 8 x 10-inch baking pan. In a large skillet, sauté shallot in oil over medium-high heat for 1 minute. Add in hazelnuts and cumin and cook another minute. Add garlic and spinach and cook another minute. Stir in quinoa and remove from heat.

Spoon quinoa mixture into bell pepper halves and lightly spray with oil. Roast at top of oven for 25–30 minutes, until lightly browned and bell peppers are softened. Serve immediately.

Wilted Spinach with Spicy Thai Peanut Vinaigrette

Makes 4 servings

A good spicy Thai peanut sauce is great drizzled on just about everything—but is an especially fabulous flavor pair with spinach.

⅓ cup peanut butter (if possible, a roasted dark variety)
¼ cup rice vinegar
4 tablespoons canola oil, divided
1 teaspoon sesame oil
3 tablespoons tamari or soy sauce
3 tablespoons agave nectar or maple syrup
½ teaspoon chile sauce
1 tablespoon grated fresh ginger
3 cloves garlic, pressed, divided
½ teaspoon kosher salt
12 cups chopped fresh spinach leaves
Salt and pepper, to taste
½ cup chopped roasted peanuts

Blend peanut butter, vinegar, 3 tablespoons canola oil, sesame oil, tamari, agave, chile sauce, ginger, half of garlic, and salt together until smooth. Set aside at room temperature for flavors to blend.

Heat a large skillet or wok to medium-high heat. Add remaining canola oil to pan, then add remaining garlic, and then spinach and stir constantly, for about 1 minute, until spinach just begins to wilt. Season with a little salt and pepper.

Arrange spinach on a serving platter. Drizzle with peanut sauce, sprinkle on peanuts, and serve immediately.

White Bean-Stuffed Tomatoes

Makes 4 servings

This hearty dish looks pretty on a platter—good enough to impress the boss!

2 slices rustic artisan-style bread

2 tablespoons olive oil, divided

1 clove garlic

2 tablespoons diced parsley

1 can (15 ounces) cannellini beans, drained and rinsed

2 tablespoons minced red onion

3 tablespoons capers

1 tablespoon sherry vinegar

Salt and pepper, to taste

4 large ripe tomatoes*

Brush bread slices with 1 tablespoon oil and broil about 6 inches from heat for 2 minutes or until lightly browned, watching closely so as not to burn. Turn bread slices over, brush with remaining oil, and broil for another 2 minutes, or until lightly browned.

Switch oven to "Bake" mode and preheat to 375 degrees.

Remove bread from oven and rub one side with garlic. Pulse bread in food processor until small crumbs. Toss bread crumbs with parsley, beans, onion, capers, and vinegar. Add salt and pepper.

Cut tops off tomatoes and scoop out tomato flesh, reserving for another use. Spoon bean mixture into hollow tomatoes. Place on a baking sheet and place tomato tops next to tomatoes.

Bake for 25–30 minutes. Serve with tops placed on tomatoes.

* For a beautiful presentation, choose tomatoes with the green vines still on tops.

Garlic Thyme White Bean Smash

Makes 6–8 servings

Mashed potatoes have met their match! This flavorful side has the same comforting feel with a healthy twist.

    2 medium shallots, diced
    3 cloves garlic, minced
    ¼ cup extra virgin olive oil, divided
    2 tablespoons minced thyme leaves or other fresh herbs
    4 cans (15 ounces each) any variety white beans, drained
        and rinsed
    1 tablespoon lemon juice
    ¼ cup water, or more as needed
    Salt and pepper, to taste
    Cayenne pepper sauce, to taste

In a large skillet, sauté the shallots and garlic over medium heat in 1 tablespoon oil for 2–3 minutes, until onion is translucent. Add thyme leaves and cook another minute. Add in beans and remaining oil and mash with potato masher. Slowly add in lemon juice and water as needed to reach a fluffy, mashed potato-type texture. Taste and add salt, pepper, and cayenne pepper sauce, as desired. Serve warm.

Green Goddess Rice

Makes 4–6 servings

You won't believe how creamy and flavorful rice can be—this is rice on a whole different level of deliciousness!

1½ cups long-grain white rice
3 cups Vegetable Broth (page 10)
2 tablespoons lime juice
1 teaspoon lime zest
1 large ripe avocado, peeled and pitted
½ cup diced cilantro or parsley leaves
1 teaspoon cayenne pepper sauce
      Water, as needed
      Salt and pepper, to taste

Bring rice and broth to a boil in a medium saucepan. Reduce heat, cover, and simmer for about 20 minutes, until rice is tender. Set aside for a few minutes and then fluff with a fork.

Place lime juice, zest, avocado, cilantro, and pepper sauce in a blender and blend, adding a little water as necessary (mixture should be the consistency of sour cream). Stir mixture into rice, taste, and add salt and pepper, if desired.

Pistachio Lemon Spaghetti Squash

Makes 4–6 servings

Jazz up mild spaghetti squash with lemon for tang and pistachios for crunch and you'll have a side dish to remember!

1 large spaghetti squash
3 tablespoons olive oil, divided
1 shallot, minced
1 clove garlic, minced
2 tablespoons minced parsley
1 teaspoon lemon zest
1 tablespoon lemon juice
Salt and pepper, to taste
¼ cup diced pistachios

Preheat oven to 375 degrees.

Bake whole squash for 30 minutes on a baking sheet. Remove from oven and cut squash in half lengthwise. Scoop out seeds in center. Brush cut sides of squash with 1 tablespoon oil. Place cut sides down on a baking sheet and return to oven to bake another 30 minutes.

While squash is baking, sauté shallot in remaining oil in a large skillet over medium-high heat for 2–3 minutes, until softened. Add garlic and cook another minute. Remove from heat and stir in parsley, lemon zest, and juice.

Remove squash from oven and separate strands of cooked squash flesh with a fork. Place in skillet and toss. Add salt and pepper to season. Stir in pistachios. Serve immediately.

Spring Asparagus Risotto

Makes 8–10 servings

Make this when asparagus is filling up the shelves at the grocery store and overflowing on tables at farmers markets for a perfect seasonal celebration.

1 pound asparagus, tough ends discarded
6 cups Vegetable Broth (page 10)
3 tablespoons olive oil, divided
1 large red onion, diced
1½ cups Arborio rice
½ cup dry white wine
8 ounces cremini mushrooms, sliced
½ cup peas
2 scallions, chopped (both white and green parts)
Salt, to taste

Chop asparagus tips off and set aside; roughly chop the rest of the stalks. Heat broth in a medium saucepan over medium heat. Add the chopped asparagus stalks and cook until soft, at least 5 minutes. Remove stalks and place in blender or food processor with ¼ cup of the broth. Purée until smooth and set aside. Reduce heat under broth to low, but keep broth hot.

In a large skillet over medium heat, warm 2 tablespoons oil. Add onion and sauté until softened, stirring occasionally, about 3–5 minutes. Add rice and cook, stirring occasionally, until well coated in the oil, 2–3 minutes. Set a timer for 15 minutes at this point. Add wine and stir until absorbed.

Now begin adding the warmed broth ½ cup at a time, stirring continuously. As soon as the liquid has been almost completely absorbed, add another ½ cup. This process will go on for about 20–25 minutes total (the timer is for adding the veggies), and while you are attending to it continuously, there's no sense of urgency either. Sauté mushrooms in another small skillet with remaining tablespoon of oil during this process.

When the timer goes off, add peas and reserved asparagus tips, continuing to add ½ cup broth as needed. Begin tasting rice at this time. It should be tender but with a bit of a crunch. When it feels just about right, stir in the asparagus purée and mushrooms. Taste and adjust seasoning, adding salt, if needed. Top with scallions and serve immediately.

Asian Green Bean Sauté
Makes 4 servings

This is a fabulous, flavor-packed side for any meal, Asian or not! It is easily adjusted to be subtly or aggressively spicy.

  1 pound green beans, ends trimmed
  2 tablespoons coconut oil
  5 cloves garlic, minced
  1 tablespoon tamari or soy sauce
  1 tablespoon rice vinegar
  ½ teaspoon chile sauce, or more to taste
  1½ tablespoons toasted sesame oil
  2 tablespoons sesame seeds
  Salt, to taste

In a medium stockpot, bring about 2 quarts water (enough to cover beans) to a boil. Add green beans and cook for 3–4 minutes, just until beans start to become tender. Immediately drain in a colander.

Heat the coconut oil in a large skillet, add garlic, and sauté for 2–3 minutes, until fragrant but not yet starting to brown. Add green beans, tossing until coated with oil and garlic. Add tamari, vinegar, and chile sauce, sautéing until liquid is reduced a bit then add the sesame oil and seeds. Taste for seasoning and add salt, if desired.

Root Beer-Braised Sweet Potatoes

Makes 4–6 servings

Yes, it's true. Root beer and sweet potatoes meet in a flavor match made in heaven!

>   2 pounds sweet potatoes, peeled
>   1 red onion, peeled
>   2 tablespoons olive oil
>   2 tablespoons apple cider vinegar
>   1 bottle (12 ounces) good quality artisan root beer (not diet)
>   Salt and pepper, to taste
>   ½ cup diced toasted hazelnuts

Cut sweet potatoes in half lengthwise and then cut into ¼-inch thick half-moon slices. Cut onion in half and then cut into ¼-inch thick half-moon slices.

Heat a large skillet to medium-high heat. Add oil and sweet potato slices. Cook for 3–5 minutes, stirring frequently, until lightly browned.

Add onion, vinegar, and root beer to skillet. Reduce to a simmer. Cover and simmer for 15–20 minutes, until sweet potatoes are fork tender. Uncover and cook another 3–5 minutes, until most of liquid has evaporated. Season with salt and pepper and sprinkle with hazelnuts.

Cherry Pecan Quinoa

Makes 4–6 servings

You just can't beat the flavor combination in this playful pilaf.

>   2 cups quinoa
>   2 cups Vegetable Broth (page 10)
>   2 cups water
>   ¼ cup balsamic vinegar
>   2 tablespoons extra virgin olive oil
>   1 tablespoon sugar
>   1 tablespoon spicy brown mustard
>   1 cup diced radicchio leaves

½ cup dried cherries, diced

½ cup chopped pecans

¼ cup diced parsley

Salt and pepper, to taste

Cook quinoa in broth and water according to package directions. Remove from heat and let stand 5 minutes. Fluff with fork, and let cool to warm.

Whisk together the vinegar, oil, sugar, and mustard and stir into quinoa. Stir in remaining ingredients. Serve warm or at room temperature.

Southern-Style Collard Greens

Makes 4–6 servings

Who needs a ham hock when you've got this flavorful recipe? Try these smokey, tender greens just once and you'll be convinced.

5 cloves garlic, chopped

3 tablespoons toasted sesame oil

1 cup Vegetable Broth (page 10)

½ cup water

2 bunches collard greens, stems removed and cut into approximately 2-inch squares

1 piece dulse (sea vegetable) or 1 teaspoon smoked salt

1 teaspoon salt (omit if using smoked salt)

1 teaspoon hot pepper sauce

¼ cup apple cider vinegar

Sauté garlic in oil in a large, heavy skillet for 3–4 minutes, until garlic starts to brown. Add broth, water, and collards, using additional water to fully immerse the greens, if necessary. Bring briefly to a boil then reduce heat to low.

Add all remaining seasonings except vinegar, cover, and let simmer for an hour and a half, periodically stirring and turning the greens. Add apple cider vinegar and serve with extra hot pepper sauce, to taste.

Cuban Pilaf Bowl with Black Beans and Plantains

Makes 4–6 servings

You'll love the variety of flavors in this easy, festive dish.

3 cups Vegetable Broth (page 10)

3 tablespoons coconut oil

1 small onion, diced

1 red bell pepper, diced

3 cloves garlic, minced

1 cup short-grain brown rice

2 medium-size ripe plantains, diced

2 cans (14 ounces each) black beans, drained and rinsed

Juice and zest of 1 lime

1 teaspoon hot pepper sauce

½ teaspoon salt

½ cup cilantro, chopped

Heat broth over medium heat in a small saucepan on a back burner. Cover to keep hot but not boiling. In a large skillet, heat the oil over medium high and cook the onion for 2 minutes; add bell pepper and garlic and cook for another 2–3 minutes, until onion and bell pepper are soft and fragrant.

Add rice into mixture, stirring until well coated in oil. Begin adding the hot broth ½ cup at a time, stirring continuously until moisture is absorbed. (You will probably only need to use about 2 cups of broth in total until the rice is cooked through, but the extra cup is good to have in case you need a little more.) After about half the broth has been added, stir in the plantain and continue the cooking process, stirring in broth in ½ cup increments.

Once rice is cooked through, add black beans, lime juice and zest, pepper sauce, salt, and cilantro, reserving a little extra cilantro for garnish. Adjust seasoning to taste and desired spiciness.

Tangy Summer Slaw with Fennel

Makes 6–8 servings

This bright, zesty, colorful salad is a welcome addition to any picnic or potluck.

1 bulb fennel, fronds removed, shredded
½ head red cabbage, cored and shredded
1 tart apple, cored and shredded
1 large carrot, grated
1 tablespoon poppy seeds
1 tablespoon sunflower seeds
Juice and zest from ½ of large grapefruit (about ¼ cup juice)
1 tablespoon maple syrup
1 teaspoon Dijon mustard
1 large shallot, minced
¼ teaspoon dried thyme (or 1 teaspoon fresh)
½ teaspoon salt
⅓ cup extra virgin olive oil
2 to 3 tablespoons chives, minced

In a large mixing bowl, mix together fennel, cabbage, apple, and carrot. Add seeds and toss well. In a small bowl, combine the grapefruit juice and zest, maple syrup, mustard, shallot, thyme, and salt then slowly whisk in the oil.

Pour grapefruit vinaigrette over the slaw and toss again to combine thoroughly. For best results, allow to chill for at least a few hours or overnight. Sprinkle with chives before serving.

Oyster Mushrooms Rockefeller

Makes 4–6 servings

Believe it or not, this classic oyster dish is even better when made with oyster mushrooms instead.

1 pound oyster mushrooms
2 tablespoons olive oil, divided
Salt and pepper, to taste
½ yellow onion, diced
½ red bell pepper, diced
1 box (10 ounces) frozen chopped
    spinach, thawed
Juice and zest of 1 lemon
3 strips Eggplant Bacon (page 14), optional
2 slices multi-grain bread
Olive oil spray

Chop the mushrooms and sauté in 1 tablespoon of oil in a large skillet over medium-high heat, until lightly browned. Remove from skillet to a serving dish. Sprinkle with salt and pepper.

In same skillet, sauté onion in remaining oil for 2 minutes over medium-high heat. Add bell pepper and cook another 2 minutes or so, until softened. Sprinkle with salt and pepper.

Squeeze spinach dry with a kitchen towel and then add to skillet with lemon juice and zest. Stir until heated through. Crumble eggplant bacon into mixture. Spoon spinach mixture over top of mushrooms in serving dish.

Pulse bread slices in a food processor until very small crumbs. Spread bread crumbs on a baking sheet and spray lightly with oil. Toast under a broiler 6 inches from heat until lightly browned. Sprinkle bread crumbs on top of dish and serve immediately.

DESSERTS AND OTHER DELIGHTS

Chocolate Decadence Cheesefake

Makes 8 servings

This vegan cheesecake is one of the most delectable desserts you'll ever try—and if you don't tell people it's vegan, they will never, ever guess.

1½ cups chocolate graham cracker crumbs
6 tablespoons vegan margarine, melted
16 ounces vegan cream cheese, softened
16 ounces silken tofu
½ teaspoon vanilla
16 ounces vegan chocolate chips, melted
⅓ cup flour
1 cup sugar

Preheat oven to 350 degrees.

Mix graham cracker crumbs and margarine together and then press into the bottom of a 9-inch springform pan that's lined with aluminum foil. Let chill in refrigerator while filling is prepared.

In a food processor or high-speed blender, combine all remaining ingredients. Pour over crust and then place pan inside a large, deep baking dish. Fill the baking dish with hot water, taking care not to disturb the springform pan inside and transfer to the oven.

Bake 50 minutes and then turn off the oven. Open the oven door and let cheesecake set for about an hour. Remove from oven and transfer pan to the refrigerator. Chill, covered, for at least 3 hours.

Secret Ingredient Chocolate Pudding

Makes 4 small servings

So rich, creamy, and decadent—no one will guess they're eating a completely raw dessert filled with some of the healthiest fat there is!

  1 ripe avocado, peeled and pitted
  ⅓ cup agave or maple syrup
  ¼ cup cocoa powder
  1 teaspoon vanilla
  1¼ teaspoons salt
  3 tablespoons nondairy milk, of choice

Blend all ingredients in a blender or food processor on high until smooth. Add a bit more liquid, if needed. Spoon into 4 small bowls or ramekins and serve.

Smokey Maple Caramel Corn

Serves 6–8

Meet your new favorite caramel corn. Smokey. Sweet. Incredibly addictive.

  ⅓ cup popcorn kernels (makes 12 cups popped)
  ⅓ cup coconut oil
  1½ cups maple syrup
  ½ teaspoon salt
  1 tablespoon smoked paprika
  2 cups chopped roasted and salted almonds

Pop the corn kernels and set aside.

In a medium saucepan, bring the coconut oil, maple syrup, salt, and paprika to a boil. Using a candy thermometer, boil without stirring until mixture reaches 250 degrees, about 10–12 minutes. Remove from heat and immediately stir in almonds.

Quickly the pour mixture over popcorn, stirring vigorously and quickly. Spread on an oiled baking sheet and let cool. Break into clumps and serve.

Raw Banana Ice Cream

Makes 2 servings

Now there's more to make with overripe bananas than just banana bread! Peel them and pop them in the freezer for a surprisingly delicious, easy, dairy- and sugar-free soft serve ice cream!

> 2 frozen bananas, cut into 2-inch slices
> 1 teaspoon vanilla
> 2 to 3 tablespoons cocoa powder, regular or dark
> Pinch of salt, optional

Place bananas into a high-speed blender or food processor, add remaining ingredients, and blend until smooth. A powerful high-speed blender will be the most effective, but any blender or processor will do, you just may need more time and possibly a tiny bit of additional liquid (nondairy milk, of choice). You may have to scrape the sides and pack it down a few times.

VARIATIONS

Add ¼ teaspoon peppermint extract and ¼ cup mini-chocolate chips if you're feeling indulgent—you've got mint chip. Add 2 to 3 tablespoons of nut butter—you've got a nut butter cup. Add almond extract in place of vanilla plus chopped pecans, to taste—you've got pralines and cream.

Cardamom Pistachio Rice Pudding

Makes 4 servings

This comfort food classic goes vegan with coconut milk—making it even more delicious!

⅔ cup basmati rice
3 cups water
2 cans (12 ounces each) coconut milk
Pinch of salt
1 teaspoon cardamom
½ cup sugar
1 teaspoon vanilla
Diced pistachios

In a heavy-bottom saucepan, bring the rice, water, coconut milk, and salt to a boil. Reduce heat to simmer so that the pudding cooks very slowly. Cover and simmer for 30–40 minutes, stirring occasionally, until mixture is thickened to the consistency of oatmeal.

Remove from heat and stir in cardamom, sugar, and vanilla. Serve chilled or at room temperature, sprinkled with pistachios on top.

Pink Lemonade Bars

Makes 8 bars

A lemon curd made with no eggs? Yes, it's possible! Try these lemon squares with a fun raspberry twist.

½ cup palm shortening
¼ cup plus 3 tablespoons powdered sugar, divided
1 cup unbleached flour
5 tablespoons coconut oil
2 tablespoons cornstarch
½ cup almond milk
¼ cup sugar
Juice and zest of 2 lemons (approximately ⅓ cup)
1½ tablespoons raspberry jam
1/8 teaspoon salt

Preheat oven to 350 degrees. Prepare an 8 x 8-inch baking pan with baking spray (or grease with shortening and sprinkle lightly with flour).

Using a handheld mixer, beat the shortening and ¼ cup powdered sugar together until well combined. Add in the flour, continuing to beat with mixer until dough resembles coarse sand. Press dough into bottom and slightly up the sides of prepared pan (dough will be crumbly). Bake for 15–20 minutes, or until lightly golden. Let cool while preparing the filling.

Place coconut oil into a small saucepan and melt over medium heat. Whisk cornstarch into almond milk in a small mixing bowl. When coconut oil has melted, slowly whisk in the almond milk mixture. Stir in sugar. Whisk in lemon juice and zest, jam, and salt. Bring to a light boil and continue cooking, whisking frequently, until sauce thickens. Cook for 3–4 more minutes then remove from heat. Let cool for a few minutes then pour over prebaked crust.

Refrigerate at least 2 hours, until chilled. Sift remaining powdered sugar over the top just before serving. Cut into 8 bars.

Classic Apple Dumplings

Makes 8 servings

Your whole house will smell homey and comforting with these delightful dumplings baking.

4 medium baking apples, such as Braeburn
2 tablespoons lemon juice
1 box (17 ounces) frozen puff pastry, thawed
⅓ cup brown sugar
2 tablespoons cornstarch
2 teaspoons cinnamon
¼ teaspoon salt
⅔ cup diced walnuts
½ tablespoon olive oil

Preheat oven to 400 degrees. Peel and core apples and then cut in half across diameter. Toss in lemon juice.

Roll out both sheets of pastry dough so that they are about 1-inch longer and wider than the original sheet size. Cut each sheet into 4 squares using a pizza cutter or knife. Place an apple half in the center of each square.

Mix together the brown sugar, cornstarch, cinnamon, and salt. Divide this mixture in half. Toss walnuts in oil. Toss oiled walnuts in half of brown sugar mixture. Stuff the center of each apple with walnut mixture. Sprinkle remaining brown sugar mixture over apples.

Bring up corners of pastry squares to the top of the apple half. Pinch shut. Pinch 4 side seams together tightly. Place on a baking sheet and bake at top of oven for 30–35 minutes, until apples are soft when a small knife is inserted and pastry is lightly browned.

Skillet Apple Crisp

Makes 6–8 servings

The classic American apple dessert goes vegan—and even more delicious than the original!

  6 large Golden Delicious apples, peeled and cut into
      ¼-inch thick slices
  ¼ cup maple syrup
  2 teaspoons cinnamon, divided
  Dash of freshly grated nutmeg
  ⅓ cup coconut oil, divided
  1 cup apple cider
  1 tablespoon lemon juice
  2 tablespoons cornstarch
  ¾ cup flour
  ¾ cup diced pecans
  ¾ cup rolled oats
  ½ cup brown sugar
  ½ teaspoon salt

Toss apple slices in maple syrup, 1 teaspoon cinnamon, and nutmeg. Let sit 20 minutes. Preheat oven to 425 degrees.

Heat a 12-inch heavy-bottom oven-proof skillet (a cast iron skillet, if possible) to medium-high heat. Add 2 tablespoons oil to skillet. Add apple mixture and sauté 12–15 minutes, stirring frequently, until apples are fork tender.

Mix together the apple cider, lemon juice, and cornstarch. Stir into skillet mixture until liquid is thickened. Remove from heat.

In a medium bowl, mix the flour, pecans, oats, brown sugar, remaining cinnamon, salt, and remaining oil together.

Crumble the oat mixture on top of skillet apple mixture. Bake at top of oven for about 20 minutes, until topping is lightly browned.

Banana Hazelnut Empanadas

Makes 8 empanadas

This five-ingredient dessert is shockingly easy to make—yet tastes like you were working in the kitchen all day!

> 1 box (17 ounces) frozen puff pastry, thawed
> 1 ripe banana, mashed into pea-size chunks
> ¼ cup vegan chocolate chips
> 1¼ cups chopped toasted hazelnuts
> 1½ cups powdered sugar

Preheat oven to 400 degrees. Spread 1 sheet of puff pastry on a lightly floured surface. Roll out slightly with a rolling pin. Cut 4 (5-inch) circles, using a small plate as a guide.

Mix banana, chocolate chips, and hazelnuts together. Spoon a generous tablespoon into the center of each circle.

Spread a little water around the edges of the puff pastry circles and then fold them in half, forming half-moon shapes. Crimp around the edges with a fork. Place empanadas on a baking sheet lined with a silicone mat or parchment paper. Repeat process for second pastry sheet, making 8 empanadas total.

Bake at top of oven for 20–25 minutes, until lightly browned. Remove from oven. Mix powdered sugar with just a little water to form a glaze and then drizzle over empanadas. Serve warm.

Peanut Butter Chocolate Chip Cookies

Makes 24 cookies

These are every bit as satisfying as both the chocolate chip and the peanut butter cookies you grew up with. Two great tastes that still taste great together!

> 2 cups flour
> 1 teaspoon baking soda
> ½ teaspoon salt
> 1 cup palm shortening
> 1 cup brown sugar
> ¾ cup unsweetened peanut butter
> 1½ teaspoons vanilla
> 2 tablespoons flax seed meal stirred into 6 tablespoons
>   hot water
> 1 cup vegan chocolate chips
> ½ cup chopped pecans, optional

Preheat oven to 350 degrees.

In a large mixing bowl, whisk together flour, baking soda, and salt. In the bowl of a stand mixer, cream together shortening and brown sugar. Reducing speed, add in peanut butter, vanilla, and flax mixture. Slowly add in dry ingredients ½ cup at a time then stir in chocolate chips and pecans, if using.

Scoop by heaping tablespoons onto a parchment paper or silicone mat-lined baking sheet, spacing evenly. Bake for 15–20 minutes, taking care not to over bake. Cool on a rack.

Home Run Oatmeal Cookies

Makes 18 cookies

These are the best oatmeal cookies you will ever make—crunchy on the outside and creamy on the inside. They will be a home run for you every single time!

8 ounces chopped (1½ cups) walnuts

4 tablespoons coconut oil

1 cup light brown sugar

½ cup water

2 teaspoons vanilla

2 cups oat flour

1 teaspoon baking soda

1 teaspoon salt

½ teaspoon cinnamon

2 cups old-fashioned rolled oats

½ cup chopped raisins or sweetened dried cranberries

Preheat oven to 375 degrees.

In a food processor or blender, blend the walnuts and oil until a very smooth walnut butter is formed, about 3 minutes, scraping down sides frequently.

Bring the brown sugar and water to a boil in a small saucepan. Remove from heat and whisk in vanilla and the walnut butter, until well blended.

Stir together the oat flour, baking soda, salt, and cinnamon. Stir dry ingredients into wet ingredients until very smooth. Add in rolled oats. Stir in raisins or cranberries. Chill dough for 30 minutes.

Using a 2-tablespoon scoop, drop dough onto a baking sheet lined with parchment paper or a silicone mat. With a wet spatula, press cookie mounds down on top, forming ⅓-inch thick cookies. Bake at top of oven for 10–12 minutes, until cookies are lightly browned and dry on top.

Pralines and Cream Custard Cups

Makes 4 servings

Try this classic ice-cream flavor in a tangy custard parfait. The praline crumbles are just as delicious as ever in dairy-free form.

> 12 Medjool dates, pitted
> ½ cup boiling water
> 1 cup whole pecans
> ¼ cup brown sugar
> 2 tablespoons regular coconut milk
> ⅛ teaspoon salt
> 2 cups vanilla coconut milk yogurt
> 1½ teaspoons vanilla
> ¼ teaspoon cinnamon

Preheat oven to 375 degrees.

Place the dates in a food processor or high-speed blender and cover with the boiling water. Let soak as you prepare the pecans.

In a small mixing bowl, stir together pecans, brown sugar, coconut milk, and salt. Spread mixture onto a baking sheet with sides that has been lined with parchment paper or a silicone mat. Bake for approximately 15–20 minutes, stirring about every 5 minutes. Remove from oven. Let cool on the pan, stirring as they cool and the coating crystallizes. Chop roughly once completely cooled.

Blend the dates until they form a paste. Add yogurt, vanilla, and cinnamon and purée until completely smooth. Spoon into 4 small custard dishes or ramekins and chill for at least 1 hour. Top each with the pecan praline topping.

Coconut Lime Gelato

Makes 6–8 servings

This tangy, creamy, no-churn ice cream is nothing short of miraculous. No special equipment necessary!

> 1 can (14 ounces) regular coconut milk
> ¼ cup coconut oil, melted
> ¼ cup lime juice (approximately 3 limes), plus zest from the juiced limes
> 1 cup sugar
> ¼ teaspoon salt

Whisk all ingredients together until completely smooth and incorporated. Pour into a shallow dish, cover with lid or plastic wrap, and freeze overnight (or at least 8 hours). For ease of serving, allow to soften slightly on the counter-top for 15 minutes (or in the refrigerator for about an hour).

Creamy Cookie Crumble Brownies

Makes 8–10 servings

Bring these to even one party, and popular demand will have you making them for every gathering thereafter.

> ¼ cup bittersweet vegan chocolate chips
> ⅓ cup coconut oil
> 2 teaspoons vanilla
> ½ cup brewed black coffee
> 8 ounces vegan cream cheese
> ¼ cup powdered sugar
> 2 cups flour
> 1 teaspoon baking powder
> 1 teaspoon salt
> 2 cups sugar
> ⅓ cup cocoa powder
> 1 cup coconut milk
> 1 cup vegan chocolate wafer cookies, crushed

In a small saucepan, combine chocolate chips, coconut oil, vanilla, and coffee. Heat until chocolate chips are melted, stirring continuously until ingredients are combined and smooth, then remove from heat and set aside to cool.

Preheat oven to 350 degrees. Grease a 9 x 12-inch baking pan liberally with vegetable shortening. In a small bowl, using a handheld electric mixer, combine the cream cheese with powdered sugar. Set this aside.

In a large mixing bowl, stir together the flour, baking powder, salt, sugar, and cocoa powder. Whisk coconut milk into cooled chocolate chip mixture then stir into dry ingredients. Pour half the batter into the prepared pan then spoon dollops of the cream cheese mixture onto the batter, spacing out evenly, reserving about ¼ cup of the cream cheese. Sprinkle with half the cookie crumbs. Cover with remaining batter then sprinkle with remaining crumbs and bake for 35–40 minutes, until a fork inserted into the center comes out clean. Let cool in pan.

Once brownies have cooled, place the reserved cream cheese mixture into a small ziplock bag and pipe a few swirls onto the top. Cut into squares and serve.

Retro Chocolate Wacky Cake

Makes 6 servings

Make a fabulous decadent cake that is a part of American History! This vegan cake recipe was popular in the hard times of the Great Depression and again in World War II, when dairy was in short supply.

    1½ cups flour
    ½ teaspoon salt
    1 teaspoon baking soda
    ¼ cup cocoa powder
    6 tablespoons vegetable oil
    1 cup sugar
    1 tablespoon white vinegar
    1 teaspoon vanilla
    1 cup water
    Powdered sugar

Preheat oven to 350 degrees.

In a large bowl, mix together the flour, salt, baking soda, and cocoa powder. In another bowl, stir together the oil, sugar, vinegar, vanilla, and water. Stir wet mixture into dry mixture.

Pour into an oiled 8 x 8-inch baking pan. Bake for about 30 minutes in center of oven, until center is set. Cool completely and dust with powdered sugar.

Variation: To make a 9 x 13-inch cake, double all ingredients and add 10 minutes to cooking time.

HAPPY HOLIDAYS AND SPECIAL OCCASIONS

My Heart Beets for You Salad

Makes 4 servings

Just three easy steps to make these yummy beet hearts, a healthy and beautiful Valentine's Day treat!

>   1 pound beets
>   Canola oil spray
>   Salt, to taste
>   8 cups chopped mixed salad greens
>   ¼ cup vinaigrette, of choice
>   ½ cup toasted chopped pecans
>   4 radishes, thinly sliced

Preheat oven to 400 degrees.

Peel and cut the beets into ¼-inch thick slices and then cut into heart shapes with a heart-shaped cookie cutter. Place on an oiled baking sheet, lightly spray with canola oil, and sprinkle with salt. Roast for about 30 minutes, or until fork tender. Let cool.

Toss remaining ingredients together and spoon onto 4 salad plates. Place beet hearts on top.

New Orleans King Cake

Makes 8 servings

This colorful Mardi Gras pastry is every bit as festively delicious in vegan form.

> 1 cup light coconut milk
>
> ¼ cup coconut oil
>
> 2 packages (¼ ounce each) active dry yeast
>
> ¾ cup warm water (110 degrees)
>
> ½ cup plus 1 tablespoon sugar, divided
>
> 2 tablespoons golden flax seed meal, stirred into ⅓ cup warm water
>
> 1 teaspoon salt
>
> ¼ teaspoon nutmeg
>
> 5½ cups flour

FILLING

> 1 cup light brown sugar
>
> 2 teaspoons cinnamon
>
> ½ cup pecans, chopped (reserve a single pecan half intact)
>
> ½ cup flour
>
> ½ cup coconut oil
>
> 1 tablespoon warm water
>
> 1 teaspoon vanilla
>
> 2 cups powdered sugar
>
> Purple, yellow, and green sugar sprinkles

In a small saucepan, bring coconut milk just to a boil then immediately remove from heat and stir in coconut oil. Set aside to cool down to room temperature. In a large bowl, dissolve yeast in water with 1 tablespoon of the sugar. Let stand approximately 10 minutes, until foamy.

Stir the cooled coconut milk mixture into yeast in the large bowl. Whisk in the flax and water mixture. Add the remaining sugar, salt, and nutmeg. Using a rubber spatula, mix the flour into the liquid 1 cup at a time. When the dough has formed into a cohesive ball, move to a floured countertop and knead until stretchy, about 5 minutes. Place in an oiled bowl, cover with a cloth, and let rise for 2 hours, until double in volume.

While pastry dough rises, make the filling. Combine brown sugar, cinnamon, chopped pecans, and flour. Melt the coconut oil and stir into sugar mixture, stirring until it's the texture of crumbly wet sand.

Once the dough has risen, punch down and divide in half. Roll both halves into large rectangles, about 10–12 inches long. Sprinkle each rectangle with half the brown sugar filling, then roll up jelly-roll style starting with the long side. Bring ends together to form a circle, pinching ends together to seal.

Using a sharp knife or scissors, make 2-inch slits about every 3 inches around each circle. Hide the intact pecan half by tucking into the dough through one of the vents. (This is traditionally a small plastic baby, pushed up into the dough once baking is finished.) Let dough rise for another ½ hour.

Preheat oven to 350 degrees. Prepare 2 baking sheets with silicone mats or parchment paper. Place each circle on its own sheet and place a ceramic ramekin or baking ring in the centers to help hold their shape. Bake for 30–40 minutes. Allow to cool just a bit before decorating (and place plastic baby from underneath, if using).

Whisk the water and vanilla into the powdered sugar and drizzle circles liberally with icing. Sprinkle alternating stripes of purple, yellow, and green sprinkles.

Note: Whoever gets the baby, whether in toy form or as represented by pecan half, is responsible for bringing the King Cake to the next Mardi Gras celebration!

Meatless Mardi Gras Muffaletta

Makes 4 servings

This Cajun classic sandwich gets a meatless makeover!

> 2 large portobello mushroom caps, sliced ¼-inch thick
> 5 tablespoons extra virgin olive oil, divided
> ½ teaspoon salt, divided
> 1 red bell pepper
> 1 cup kalamata olives, finely chopped
> 2 stalks celery, diced
> 3 cloves garlic, minced
> 2 tablespoons capers
> ¼ cup flat-leaf parsley, chopped
> 2 tablespoons red wine vinegar
> 1 teaspoon cayenne pepper sauce
> 1 large baguette
> 4 to 5 strips Eggplant Bacon (page 14), optional

Preheat oven to 425 degrees. Toss the mushroom slices in 2 tablespoons oil and ¼ teaspoon salt. Spread parchment paper or a silicone mat over a baking sheet and place mushroom slices in a single layer. Roast for about 5–7 minutes, until tender and starting to brown. Remove from oven and set aside to cool.

Roast the red pepper simply by holding it over a gas burner with tongs until skin is blackened. You can also do this by broiling it on the top rack of your oven; this will take about 5–10 minutes (check frequently). Once the skin is blackened, seal the pepper into a ziplock bag and allow the heat to steam for a few minutes. The skin should then rub off easily. Allow to cool as you assemble the rest of the salad.

Combine olives, celery, garlic, capers, and parsley in a medium bowl. In a small bowl, slowly stream remaining oil into the vinegar, whisking briskly. Stir in cayenne pepper sauce and remaining salt then pour over olive mixture and toss. Dice the cooled peppers and stir into olive salad. (Olive salad may be made a day or two ahead of time.)

Slice the baguette in half and then scoop out most of the softest inner bread. Spread the olive salad over both sides of the baguette, filling the channels you've scooped out. Place the mushrooms and bacon over the salad and close the sandwich. Press down on the top to condense the filling and bread. Wrap tightly in plastic wrap and refrigerate for at least 3 hours before serving.

Luck O' the Irish Colcannon

Makes 6–8 servings

Add this creamy comfort food classic to your St. Patrick's Day celebration.

2 pounds Yukon gold potatoes,
    approximately 6 large, quartered
¼ cup white vinegar
1 large bunch kale, washed, stemmed,
    and coarsely chopped
1 tablespoon olive oil
1 large onion, diced
1 cup Vegetable Broth (page 10)
⅛ teaspoon fresh nutmeg
Salt and freshly ground pepper, to taste

Cover potatoes with salted water and vinegar in a large stockpot and bring to a boil. Boil for 10 minutes and then add the kale and cook for another 10 minutes. Drain into a colander and return empty pot to the stove.

Add oil and reduce heat to medium high. When oil is hot, add onion and sauté until softened and starting to brown a little. Add potatoes and kale back to the pot then stir in the broth and mash to your preferred consistency. Season with nutmeg, and add salt and pepper.

Potato Leek Soup with Shamrock Croutons

Makes 6–8 servings

If you're lucky, you'll enjoy crunchy, toasty shamrocks floating on creamy potato leek soup—a leprechaun's delight!

SOUP

1 large leek
1 cup sliced white button mushrooms
2 tablespoons canola oil
4 cups Vegetable Broth (page 10)
1 pound russet potatoes, peeled and cut in 2-inch chunks
1 tablespoon white wine vinegar
Salt and pepper, to taste

SHAMROCKS

4 slices thin, firm bread
¼ cup Vegan Pesto (page 12)

Cut leek in half lengthwise and then into ¼-inch thick half-moon slices. Sauté leeks and mushrooms in oil in a stockpot until tender, about 5 minutes. Stir in broth and potatoes and bring to a boil. Reduce heat and simmer uncovered for about 20 minutes, until potatoes are tender.

Blend soup with a stick blender or in a regular blender in batches until very smooth. Add in vinegar and salt and pepper. Serve soup hot with shamrocks on the side for diners to float on top of their soup.

To make the Shamrocks, cut bread slices into small shamrock shapes with a cookie cutter, or cut into squares. Spread a thin layer of pesto on bread pieces and then broil until bread is lightly browned around edges.

The Easter Bunny's Favorite Soup

Makes 6–8 servings

This enlightened carrot soup is made even more flavorful with a swirl of pesto made from the carrot tops.

1 medium yellow onion, diced
6 tablespoons olive oil, divided
1½ pounds carrots with tops
2 tablespoons grated fresh ginger
6 cloves garlic, 4 minced
1 can (14 ounces) coconut milk
6 cups Vegetable Broth (page 10)
1 tablespoon white wine vinegar
¼ cup toasted chopped walnuts
1 teaspoon kosher salt
Cayenne pepper sauce, to taste

In a large stockpot, sauté the onion in 2 tablespoons oil over medium-high heat for 2–3 minutes, until softened.

Remove tops from carrots, chop, and set aside. Peel carrots and cut into ¼-inch slices. Add carrots, ginger, and minced garlic to onion mixture and cook 15 minutes, until softened and starting to brown. Add the coconut milk, broth, and vinegar. Bring to a boil and then reduce the heat to low and let simmer for 30 minutes, uncovered.

While soup is simmering, process in food processor or blender the remaining oil, remaining garlic, walnuts, and carrot tops; set aside.

Blend soup with a stick blender or in a regular blender in batches. Add salt and cayenne pepper sauce. Let simmer another 20 minutes. Strain through a fine mesh strainer and serve warm, with a spoonful of carrot top pesto swirled in before serving.

Rice Ball Jack-O'-Lantern Bites

Makes 12 bites

Halloween treats don't have to be sugary sweet—these delicious little rice balls are fun, festive, and flavorful.

> 1½ cups medium- or short-grain rice
> 2 cups carrot juice
> 1 cup Vegetable Broth (page 10)
> ½ teaspoon salt
> Black olives
> Green bell pepper or fresh green beans

In a medium saucepan, combine rice, carrot juice, broth, and salt and bring to a boil. Cover, reduce heat, and simmer for 15 minutes, or until all liquid is absorbed. Let cool to room temperature.

To make jack-o'-lanterns, form approximately 1-inch balls out of rice, pressing firmly with hands. If rice sticks to hands, lightly sprinkle hands with water when rolling.

To form eyes and mouths, cut black olives into shapes and press into the rice balls. To make stem, cut a small triangle of green bell pepper and stick into rice ball on top or snip off the tips of fresh green beans to use as a stem.

Thanksgiving Stuffed Acorn Squash

Makes 8 servings

The pomegranate seeds are juicy little jewels in this Moroccan-inspired, highly nutritious side dish, adding tart little bursts of flavor that pair beautifully with the mellow, sweet spice of the stuffing.

> 4 acorn squash
> 3 tablespoons olive oil, divided
> 1½ teaspoons each salt and freshly ground pepper, divided
> ½ cup water
> 2 cups Vegetable Broth (page 10)
> 1 teaspoon salt, plus more to taste
> 1 cup quinoa
> 2 bay leaves
> ½ cup pine nuts or coarsely chopped cashews
> 1 onion, diced
> 8 ounces cremini or white button mushrooms, sliced
> 2 cloves garlic, minced
> ½ teaspoon cinnamon
> ¼ teaspoon cardamom
> Pinch of ground cloves
> Zest of 1 lemon
> ½ cup currants
> Seeds of 1 pomegranate (about 1 cup), divided

Preheat oven to 375 degrees.

Cut squashes in half, scooping out the seeds, and brush with 1 tablespoon oil. Season with about ½ teaspoon salt and pepper. Place face down on a roasting pan, pouring water into the reservoir below the rack (you could also use a wire cooling rack in a large baking dish or a rimmed baking sheet to elevate the squash). Bake for 30–35 minutes, until tender.

While squash is baking, bring the broth to a boil in a small saucepan. Add quinoa and bay leaves then reduce heat to a low simmer. Cover and cook for 15 minutes, until all liquid is absorbed. Remove from heat, fluff with a fork, and discard bay leaves; set quinoa aside.

Heat a large dry skillet and toast the nuts, shaking pan frequently, until golden and fragrant. Remove nuts to let cool. Add remaining oil to the skillet, and over medium heat, sauté onion until soft and translucent. Add mushrooms, garlic, cinnamon, cardamom, and cloves. Stir for about 5 minutes, until mushrooms have softened. Transfer mushroom mixture and quinoa to a large mixing bowl and add the nuts, lemon zest, currants, remaining salt and pepper, and a bit more than half the pomegranate seeds. Mix well and adjust seasonings.

Turn squashes over so they're cut-side up and reposition on rack in roasting pan or baking dish. Scoop filling into cavities of each, piling it high. Bake for 20 minutes. Top with remaining pomegranate seeds.

Pumpkin Crème Brûlée

Makes 4 servings

Familiar flavors get an elegant and delicious twist in this easy variation on classic pumpkin pie.

 1 can (14 ounces) regular coconut milk
 1 teaspoon vanilla
 2 teaspoons lemon juice
 1 teaspoon pumpkin pie spice
 ½ teaspoon cinnamon
 ¼ teaspoon salt
 ½ cup pumpkin purée
 ¼ cup brown sugar
 ¼ cup sugar plus 6 heaping teaspoons, divided
 2 tablespoons low- or no-sugar pectin

Chill 4 small ramekins in refrigerator until ready to use. In a large bowl, combine all ingredients except the 6 teaspoons sugar and the pectin. Whisk until smooth. Pour into a medium saucepan and heat to a rolling boil. Slowly whisk in pectin and continue boiling for 3 minutes, whisking continuously.

Remove from heat and let cool for a few minutes before pouring into chilled ramekins. Place in refrigerator until set, at least 2–3 hours. Immediately before serving, sprinkle 1 heaping teaspoon of sugar over each ramekin, distributing as evenly as possible. Caramelize the sugar with a culinary torch (following all manufacturer's instructions), moving the flame continuously over the surface in small circles. It will first melt into small bubbles and then harden into a smooth crust. Allow a few minutes to cool just before serving.

Alternate method for caramelizing sugar if blowtorch is not available: Just before serving, preheat broiler to high and move oven rack to the top position. Prepare ramekins with sugar as per above, place ramekins on a baking sheet, and broil until sugar melts and browns. Make sure to keep oven door cracked open in order to prevent the crème itself from heating.

Fire and Ice and Everything Spiced Holiday Nuts
Makes 6 heaping cups

This is a perennial holiday hit and the talk of any party you bring them to!

> 6 cups mixed raw nuts
> 2 teaspoons of each Chinese five-spice powder, cinnamon, cumin
> 1 teaspoon of each Chipotle chile powder (or smoked paprika), ground ginger, garlic powder, kosher salt
> ¼ cup brown sugar
> ⅓ cup extra virgin olive oil
> ¼ cup maple syrup
> ½ teaspoon cayenne pepper sauce
> ¼ cup crystallized ginger, minced
> ½ cup dried cranberries, diced

Preheat oven to 325 degrees and line 2 baking sheets with parchment paper.

Spread the nuts on baking sheets and roast for 13–15 minutes. Meanwhile, stir all spices, salt, and brown sugar together in a small bowl. In a medium bowl, combine the oil, maple syrup, and cayenne pepper sauce.

Remove nuts from oven and stir into the oil mixture. Add the spices and toss thoroughly. Return the coated nuts to the baking sheets, making sure they are in a single layer, and roast for another 5 minutes. Remove from oven and toss with crystallized ginger and cranberries. Spread out to cool.

Joy to the World Balls

Makes 60 candies

This version of our four-generation Christmas candy will remind you of a famous candy bar!

8 ounces sweetened coconut

½ cup regular coconut milk

2 pounds powdered sugar

½ cup coconut oil, melted

2 cups chopped toasted almonds

1 tablespoon vanilla

1 tablespoon palm shortening

12 ounces vegan semisweet chocolate chips

In a large bowl with a large sturdy spoon, stir together coconut, coconut milk, powdered sugar, coconut oil, almonds, and vanilla. The mixture will be very thick! Cover and refrigerate for at least 2 hours.

Remove coconut mixture from refrigerator and roll into balls using 1 tablespoon of mixture per ball.

In a double boiler, melt shortening over simmering water. Slowly stir in chocolate until melted and keep over very low heat. Using a sturdy toothpick, dip balls into chocolate and then place on a sheet of wax paper to cool.

Santa's Choice Hot Cocoa

Makes 4 servings

Leave some cookies and this drink for Santa, and you just might get extra treats!

    1 can (14 ounces) regular coconut milk
    1 can (14 ounces) light coconut milk
    2 tablespoons cocoa powder
    1 teaspoon peppermint extract
    ¼ cup vegan chocolate syrup, or more to taste
    ¼ teaspoon salt
    Vegan Whipped Cream (page 11), optional
    Crushed peppermint candies, optional

Place coconut milks in a small saucepan; whisk in cocoa powder. Bring to a simmer over medium heat and add in peppermint extract, syrup, and salt. Garnish with whipped cream and candies, as desired.

Vegan Nog

Makes 4–6 servings

Forget drinking raw eggs! This vegan version of the classic Christmas beverage is even better than the old-school version.

    2 cups raw cashews
    4 cups cold vanilla almond milk, divided
    ¼ cup maple syrup
    2 teaspoons vanilla
    ¼ teaspoon freshly grated nutmeg
    Pinch of salt
    Vegan Whipped Cream (page 11)

Cover cashews in boiling water and let soak for at least 30 minutes, until softened. Drain cashews and place in blender with 2 cups almond milk. Blend until smooth. Add remaining ingredients and blend again. Serve with whipped cream.

Magical Reindeer Droppings

Makes 12 droppings

If your family likes creative (and delicious) pranks, these easy no-bake cookies can serve as more evidence of Santa's appearance.

½ cup coconut oil
2 cups sugar
½ cup nondairy milk of choice
4 tablespoons cocoa powder
1 teaspoon vanilla
1 cup rolled oats
1 cup shredded coconut
½ cup cashews
½ cup nut butter, of choice
1 to 2 teaspoons each red and green sprinkles

Melt coconut oil in a small saucepan over medium heat. Add sugar and stir until dissolved. Add milk and cocoa powder and bring to a gentle boil for about 2–3 minutes. Remove from heat and add vanilla. Stir in oats, coconut, cashews, nut butter, and sprinkles.

While still warm, scoop into mounds on a baking sheet lined with wax paper and chill until set. Alternately, you can roll them into "log" shapes or into small pellets presented in little piles, if you feel that's more what reindeer "treats" would look like. Present as hilariously as possible.

INDEX

Donna and Anne are a reunited birth mother and daughter who discovered a common bond in the kitchen. After teaming up on their first Gibbs Smith cookbook, *101 Things To Do With Tofu*, they found they enjoyed working together so much that they created the blog Fab Frugal Food. This eventually grew into the current Apron Strings blog where they continue to create recipes and sometimes share memories and stories of reconnecting through their mutual love of food and cooking, **www.apronstringsblog.com**.

Donna Kelly is the author of two books, *French Toast* and *Quesadillas*, published by Gibbs Smith, and coauthor of four other cookbooks. When she isn't cooking and developing recipes, she is hard at work as an attorney. She is currently the Sexual Assault and Domestic Violence Resource Prosecutor for the Utah Attorney General's Office. She has four other children, three granddaughters, and lives in Provo, Utah, with her husband.

After growing up in Colorado, **Anne Tegtmeier** graduated magna cum laude from the Boston Conservatory, where she received her BFA in dance. Since 2001 she has also worked as a licensed massage therapist. Anne has spent many years as a vegetarian and is a passionate amateur cook. She is currently enrolled in Birthingway College of Midwifery's very first Associate Degree program in Lactation Science, in preparation to become an IBCLC (International Board Certified Lactation Consultant). Anne resides in Portland, Oregon, with her daughter, Lily.

Metric Conversion Chart

Volume Measurements		Weight Measurements		Temperature Conversion	
U.S.	**Metric**	**U.S.**	**Metric**	**Fahrenheit**	**Celsius**
1 teaspoon	5 ml	1/2 ounce	15 g	250	120
1 tablespoon	15 ml	1 ounce	30 g	300	150
1/4 cup	60 ml	3 ounces	90 g	325	160
1/3 cup	75 ml	4 ounces	115 g	350	180
1/2 cup	125 ml	8 ounces	225 g	375	190
2/3 cup	150 ml	12 ounces	350 g	400	200
3/4 cup	175 ml	1 pound	450 g	425	220
1 cup	250 ml	2 1/4 pounds	1 kg	450	230